Lita

MW01697721

LIVING & GIVING GOD'S DREAM

Dale O'S

DALE A. O'SHIELDS

COR
PUBLISHING

Published in Gaithersburg, Maryland, by COR Publishing.

ISBN: 978-0-9898891-8-6

Learn more about the author at www.DaleOShields.com.

Printed in the United States of America

TABLE OF CONTENTS

Introduction 5

God's D-R-E-A-M 7

Develop Your Character 39

[Be] Responsible 61

[Be] Extraordinary in Your Service 89

Align With the Team 113

Multiply Yourself 143

INTRODUCTION

This book is for the people who want to discover their God-given gifts and use them for greater impact in their local church. It's for the person who wants to be a go-to person, a true Kingdom helper and advancer. Yes, this book is for *you*.

There's never been a better time to serve God and his church than now. There have never been greater opportunities to make a difference with your life than now. Your investment in God's Kingdom has never been needed more than now.

I'm thrilled that you're taking the time to prepare and equip yourself to be all you can be for God. Let's learn how to work together with God and others to accomplish the mission of building and growing his church.

My prayer is that this book will help you in your journey toward serving God with excellence and enthusiasm!

~ *Dale A. O'Shields*

Chapter 1

God's D-R-E-A-M

God has a dream. And he wants you on his team!

God's dream is to build his church so that every person from every tribe, tongue, and nation will be with him for eternity. God's dream is to reach every person with the gospel of Jesus. His desire is clear, "God wants everyone to be saved and to know the whole truth" (1 Timothy 2:4 CEV).

God wants you to embrace his dream. He also wants you on his team, because it takes a team to fulfill his dream. Our calling is to "*live his dream*" and to "*give his dream*" to others. Life in his Kingdom is never about our dream; it's about learning and living God's dream, and sharing his dream with others.

Throughout my years of ministry, I've had the privilege of watching many people take God's dream seriously. As we've worked together, we've experienced the satisfaction of seeing God's Kingdom advanced, the fulfillment of using our gifts for God's glory, and the blessing of growing into bigger people through serving others.

Serving Others Ministers to Them . . . and Changes *You*

Over thirty years ago, my wife and I, along with our two young daughters, moved to Gaithersburg, Maryland, to begin a new church. We knew no one in the community. We were simply responding to a confirmed and affirmed call from God to plant a strong, healthy local church. It was an exciting adventure of faith, peppered with fear! We didn't know what to expect. Our goal was simple—gather people who needed Jesus and wanted to grow in their journey with him. It's been an exciting and rewarding process. To see people open their lives to Jesus, develop their personal faith in him, and begin serving others has been thrilling. There's nothing like watching people connect with one another in the local church and work together to advance God's Kingdom!

Over and over again, I'm reminded that every person has something to give. And every person is *needed* to get the work of the church done.

Serving in Any Area of the Church Is the Equivalent of Leadership

There's a famous story about a church service that took place in an old-school revival tent in a North Carolina town in 1934. A couple of young teenagers heard music and came to see what was happening. Realizing that it was a church service, they decided to leave. Before they could exit, a kind usher greeted them and invited them to a seat. That evening, they listened to a preacher named Mordecai Ham present the gospel. At the end of the message, they both received Jesus Christ as their Lord and Savior. One of them was named Billy. The other was Grady. Several years later they launched the Billy Graham Evangelistic Association, and the rest is history.

Who led those teenagers to Christ? The speaker? Perhaps. But had it not been for an usher's encouragement, they would never have heard the message. That usher made a difference for eternity! He helped lead these two young men to Jesus, and affected the eternal destiny of millions, simply by faithfully doing what he was called to do.

Leadership is all about using one's influence positively. Serving well in *any* capacity is a part of leadership. This is one of the most important principles of serving. From directing traffic in the church parking lot to cleaning the toys in the nursery, serving in the church is a vital part of spiritual leadership. It's one way you can use your life to influence others for God and good.

As you serve, you grow. Your skills grow. Your positive influence grows. Your faith grows. You get "bigger" when you give of yourself. Serving not only benefits others, it's good for you, too. It helps you discover your purpose and become the person God created you to be.

Loving the Church Is Part of Loving Jesus

Serving God and people begins with an understanding of some basics. I love the story of Vince Lombardi, the great football coach for the Green Bay Packers. He would begin every practice season by gathering his big, strapping professional football players together for some basic training—all of whom had played football from the time they were little kids and many of whom had played in the NFL for years. His first teaching session started with him holding up a football and declaring to the team, "Gentlemen, this is a football."

He made clear from the very beginning that great football was all about knowing the fundamentals. In the same way, when we understand some fundamentals of church life, it makes a big impact on our effectiveness and fulfillment. We need to start with the basics.

For as long as I can remember, church has been a key part of my life. I'm a pastor's kid, so I was in church multiple times every week all through my childhood. My family was a "church family" and my friends were "church friends." As I grew, I never quit the church. I never gave up on the church. Somehow, likely through the influence of my parents, I understood that loving the church was part of loving Jesus.

One day over 2,000 years ago, Jesus took his disciples to a place in northern Israel called Caesarea Philippi. I've visited this lovely, resort-like environment in the foothills of Mount Hermon, at the ancient Banias Spring. The atmosphere is so refreshing. It was a beautiful place for Jesus to teach his students.

In this setting, Jesus asked his followers some important questions. First, Jesus wanted to know what others were saying about him.

This question led to a more targeted and penetrating one. He wanted to know what his disciples really thought about him:

> When Jesus came to the region of Caesarea Philippi, he asked his disciples, "Who do people say the Son of Man is?" They replied, "Some say John the Baptist; others say Elijah; and still others, Jeremiah or one of the prophets." "But what about you?" he asked. "Who do you say I am?" (Matthew 16:13-15 NIV)

The last question stimulated an immediate response from Peter. For once, Peter was spot on in his answer. With the clarity that can only come through divine revelation, Peter answered Jesus' question:

> Simon Peter answered, "You are the Messiah, the Son of the living God." Jesus replied, "Blessed are you, Simon son of Jonah, for this was not revealed to you by flesh and blood, but by my Father in heaven. And I tell you that you are Peter, and on this rock I will build my church, and the gates of Hades will not overcome it." (Matthew 16:16-18 NIV)

Jesus was thrilled with Peter's response. Through an understanding that only God could give, Peter affirmed his faith in Jesus as the Messiah and Son of God. Following Peter's declaration, Jesus gave a promise to all his disciples that still stands today. Jesus promised that he would build something called "his church" with people who had the same understanding as Peter.

Before we look at what Jesus was saying about his church in this passage, let's look at what he wasn't saying. Jesus wasn't making Peter the "head" apostle of the church. Jesus wasn't saying to Peter, "I am building the church on *you*." From all we know about Peter, that would have been disastrous. Instead, Jesus was saying, "I am building the church on *the revelation Peter has about me.*"

The church is made up of people who have a life-changing, genuine understanding and faith in who Jesus really is—the Messiah and Son of God. Anybody who sincerely believes that Jesus is who he says he is becomes a part of this divine institution called the church. With that clarification, let's look at that statement again.

Jesus basically said, "*I will build my church on this rock of understanding that I am the Christ, the Son of God.*" Think of it! Jesus said, "*I will build my church.*" He gave the promise that he would be the initiator and master builder of "his church."

The Greek word for church is *ecclesia*. Maybe you recognize this word. We get our English terms ecclesiastical and ecclesiology from this root. It basically means "people who have been called out and called together for a purpose." In the spiritual context, Jesus promised to call people out of the darkness of the world and of sin to a relationship with himself and with fellow believers, and give them a purpose to accomplish together.

Jesus' church would be an organization—something with structure, a mission, and clear focus. It would also be organic—built with people who believed in him and had surrendered their lives to him. The church would be solid, fixed, and secure as well as flexible and responsive to the influence of the Holy Spirit and the needs of an ever-changing world. Organized and organic.

Jesus declared that he would build something on earth that would reflect heaven—something that would help bring heaven to earth. Jesus promised to build something that would bring his people together as a force, a team, a body, an identified group that would impact the world for God and for good. The church exists not only to get people to heaven but to get heaven to people!

That day over 2,000 years ago, in the remote environment of Caesarea Philippi, Jesus started something that's unstoppable. Although Jesus would return to heaven after his crucifixion and resurrection, his work on earth would not stop. After his ascension, on the day of Pentecost, Jesus sent the Holy Spirit to a small gathering of 120 faithful believers in an upper room in Jerusalem. Something powerful and world shaping was birthed that day—"his church" (Acts 1:15; Acts 2:1-4). From that day forward, followers of Jesus wouldn't operate as independent agents, but as members of a vital, Holy Spirit-empowered group, connected and committed to Jesus and to one another.

This is the church! It's people who know Jesus personally and live and work for God's Kingdom corporately, in relationship with one another, as a part of a team—God's team!

Ten Things You Need to Know about the Church

This makes the church very important in the plan of God. Without understanding what the church is and why the church exists, we miss a significant part of the way God works in the world.

Remember Vince Lombardi and the football analogy? Let me be a coach for a moment. Here are ten things you need to know about the church that will help you appreciate it more deeply and serve it more effectively:

1. The Church Is All Believers Everywhere Who Know Jesus Christ as Savior and Lord

The church is big. It's made up of Christian believers all around the world. This is usually referred to as the "universal church"—all believers everywhere. Anywhere around the world, you will find believers in Jesus Christ. Even though you may not speak the same language, when you meet them, you immediately know that you're family!

Then there are "local" churches. The "universal church" is expressed and experienced in local gatherings of believers in communities around the world. These faith communities are called to worship together, grow together, and serve together.

Take a look at how the Bible refers to local churches in the first century:

To all in Rome who are loved by God and called to be his holy people: Grace and peace to you from God our Father and from the Lord Jesus Christ. (Romans 1:7 NIV)

Paul, an apostle of Christ Jesus by the will of God, and Timothy our brother, To the church of God in Corinth, together with all his holy people throughout Achaia. (2 Corinthians 1:1 NIV)

Paul, an apostle—sent not from men nor by a man, but by Jesus Christ and God the Father, who raised him from the dead—and all the brothers and sisters with me, To the churches in Galatia. (Galatians 1:1, 2 NIV)

Paul, an apostle of Christ Jesus by the will of God, To God's holy people in Ephesus, the faithful in Christ Jesus. (Ephesians 1:1 NIV)

Paul and Timothy, servants of Christ Jesus, To all God's holy people in Christ Jesus at Philippi, together with the overseers and deacons. (Philippians 1:1 NIV)

To God's holy people in Colossae, the faithful brothers and sisters in Christ: Grace and peace to you from God our Father. (Colossians 1:2 NIV)

Paul, Silas and Timothy, To the church of the Thessalonians in God the Father and the Lord Jesus Christ: Grace and peace to you. (1 Thessalonians 1:1 NIV)

Being a part of the church means that we're a part of God's team. We're part of his family all around the world. We belong together. We're working for the same Lord and the same mission. Not only do we share a common commitment and work here on earth, but we're connected together for eternity!

2. You Cannot Separate Jesus from His Church

Some people want to separate Jesus from the church. They say things like, "I love Jesus, but I don't like church." Sorry, but it doesn't work that way! To love Jesus, you must also love his church. While Jesus is the "head of the church," the head functions with a body, and the church is his body. Head and body go together. You can't love the head and hate the body!

> And he is the head of the body, the church; he is the beginning and the firstborn from among the dead, so that in everything he might have the supremacy. (Colossians 1:18 NIV)

> Now you are the body of Christ, and each one of you is a part of it. (1 Corinthians 12:27 NIV)

You cannot separate Jesus from his church. Jesus and the church go together.

3. Local Churches Are Key to God's Plan for Reaching the World

Jesus is the hope of the world and Jesus is expressed through his church, so it's also appropriate to say that the church is the hope of the world. In every community, the mission of the church is to communicate the hope Jesus gives.

Most people who come to faith in Jesus Christ do so in the atmosphere of the local church. While other evangelistic outreaches and ministries are important, nothing compares to the positive impact of a Holy Spirit-filled, life-giving local church in a community. Look at what the apostle Paul said of the power of the church:

> God's purpose in all this was to use the church to display his wisdom in its rich variety to all the unseen rulers and authorities in the heavenly places. This was his eternal plan, which he carried out through Christ Jesus our Lord ... Now all glory to God, who is able, through his mighty power at work within us, to accomplish infinitely more than we might ask or think. Glory to him in the church and in Christ Jesus through all generations forever and ever! Amen. (Ephesians 3:10, 11, 20, 21 NLT)

4. To Love Jesus, We Must Also Love What Jesus Loves, and Jesus Loves His Church

If you say, "I love Jesus," then you must also say, "I love what Jesus loves." Jesus loves his church—so much so that he calls her his "bride" and laid down his life for her. So if you say, "I love Jesus" you must add, "and I love his church!"

> Husbands, love your wives, just as Christ loved the church and gave himself up for her to make

> her holy, cleansing her by the washing with water through the word, and to present her to himself as a radiant church, without stain or wrinkle or any other blemish, but holy and blameless. (Ephesians 5:25-27 NIV)

5. To Flourish, We Need to Be Planted in a Local Church

When you received Jesus Christ into your life, you became a part of the universal church. You're immediately a part of God's family. You don't have to "join" a specific church to be part of God's church. But if you're going to grow, you need to be planted in a local church.

Being planted in God's house is a key to blessings in your life.

> Planted in the house of the Lord, they will flourish in the courts of our God. They will still bear fruit in old age, they will stay fresh and green. (Psalm 92:13, 14 NIV)

Being an active part of a local church keeps you strong in your faith, increases your love for others and helps you use your life to do good:

> And let us consider how we may spur one another on toward love and good deeds, not giving up meeting together, as some are in the habit of doing, but encouraging one another—and all the more as you see the Day approaching. (Hebrews 10:24, 25 NIV)

You need to be planted in a church. Your growth depends on it. You need to get *into* good spiritual soil and *stay* there. When you're planted, you develop strong spiritual roots and start producing healthy spiritual fruit.

Does God transplant people from one local church to another one? Yes, from time to time. There are church transplants, but they're not the norm. God wants to place you in a local church and give you some roots so you can be a blessing and produce long-term fruit.

You need to be a part of a spiritual family *somewhere.*

6. The Church Has a Mission to Fulfill That Can't Be Fulfilled without Workers

The church has a job to do—a mission to fulfill. How is the mission of the church accomplished? Through people! Yes, church is work—Kingdom work, eternal work, life-changing work, but it's still work. Work doesn't get done without workers.

What's our assignment?

> Therefore go and make disciples of all nations, baptizing them in the name of the Father and of the Son and of the Holy Spirit, and teaching them to obey everything I have commanded you. And surely I am with you always, to the very end of the age. (Matthew 28:19, 20 NIV)

> After this the Lord appointed seventy-two others and sent them two by two ahead of him to every town

> and place where he was about to go. He told them, "The harvest is plentiful, but the workers are few. Ask the Lord of the harvest, therefore, to send out workers into his harvest field." (Luke 10:1, 2 NIV)
>
> You did not choose me, but I chose you and appointed you so that you might go and bear fruit—fruit that will last—and so that whatever you ask in my name the Father will give you. (John 15:16 NIV)

The church has work to do, and this means that workers are needed.

7. The Fulfillment of the Church's Mission Requires a Positive, Kingdom-Minded Culture

Work is always done in an environment. The work atmosphere or culture determines how much work gets done, the quality of the work that is done, and the thoughts and feelings of the workers doing the work. The fulfillment of the church's mission is affected by the environment in which it's executed.

Jesus talked to his disciples about culture—a lot. The Sermon on the Mount is all about culture. A great place to review Jesus' Kingdom culture manual is in the gospel of Matthew, chapters 5-7. In these chapters, Jesus taught us how we're to treat one another, how to forgive, how to deal with anger, how to bless people that try to harm us. He laid out the attitudes and behaviors that are acceptable and unacceptable in his Kingdom. *Everything* in the Sermon on the Mount is about culture. Jesus makes clear the kind of environment we need to have in our lives and in his church if it's to properly reflect the atmosphere of heaven.

Why is culture so important? Because culture always impacts mission. When you get the *culture* right, it's more likely that you'll get the *mission* right. If the culture is diseased or toxic, the mission will be affected. The church is not just about a mission; it's also about a culture—a Jesus-prescribed set of attitudes and actions that bring some of heaven to earth.

Here are just a few reminders of what church culture should look and be like:

> Jesus called them together and said, "You know that those who are regarded as rulers of the Gentiles lord it over them, and their high officials exercise authority over them. Not so with you. Instead, whoever wants to become great among you must be your servant, and whoever wants to be first must be slave of all. For even the Son of Man did not come to be served, but to serve, and to give his life as a ransom for many." (Mark 10:42-45 NIV)
>
> Don't just pretend that you love others: really love them. Hate what is wrong. Stand on the side of the good. Love each other with brotherly affection and take delight in honoring each other. Never be lazy in your work, but serve the Lord enthusiastically. Be glad for all God is planning for you. Be patient in trouble, and prayerful always. When God's children are in need, you be the one to help them out. And get into

the habit of inviting guests home for dinner or, if they need lodging, for the night. If someone mistreats you because you are a Christian, don't curse him; pray that God will bless him. When others are happy, be happy with them. If they are sad, share their sorrow. Work happily together. Don't try to act big. Don't try to get into the good graces of important people, but enjoy the company of ordinary folks. And don't think you know it all! Never pay back evil for evil. Do things in such a way that everyone can see you are honest clear through. Don't quarrel with anyone. Be at peace with everyone, just as much as possible. (Romans 12:9-18 TLB)

See what great love the Father has lavished on us, that we should be called children of God! And that is what we are! The reason the world does not know us is that it did not know him. (1 John 3:1 NIV)

Dear friends, let us love one another, for love comes from God. Everyone who loves has been born of God and knows God. Whoever does not love does not know God, because God is love. This is how God showed his love among us: He sent his one and only Son into the world that we might live through him. This is love: not that we loved God, but that he loved us and sent his Son as an atoning sacrifice for our sins. Dear friends, since God so loved us, we also ought to love one another. (1 John 4:7-11 NIV)

Therefore, as God's chosen people, holy and dearly loved, clothe yourselves with compassion, kindness,

> humility, gentleness and patience. Bear with each other and forgive one another if any of you has a grievance against someone. Forgive as the Lord forgave you. And over all these virtues put on love, which binds them all together in perfect unity. Let the peace of Christ rule in your hearts, since as members of one body you were called to peace. And be thankful. Let the message of Christ dwell among you richly as you teach and admonish one another with all wisdom through psalms, hymns, and songs from the Spirit, singing to God with gratitude in your hearts. And whatever you do, whether in word or deed, do it all in the name of the Lord Jesus, giving thanks to God the Father through him. (Colossians 3:12-17 NIV)

Building and keeping the right culture is a key to a healthy, strong local church.

8. Fulfilling the Church's Mission Requires Strong, Systematic Activities and Ministries

Here's a quick summary of some of what we've learned so far. As believers, we love Jesus, and because we love Jesus, we love his church. Because we love his church, we accept our assignment to become a worker in his church, demonstrating the right attitudes and actions.

But what is the work of the church? What's our job? What things do we need to do and do well?

There are at least eight parts of church work—eight things the church needs to do and do well. Your gifts can be used to help accomplish these important responsibilities:

- ***First, the Church Attracts***

  Attract: "to cause (someone) to choose to do or be involved in something"[1]

We cannot reach people for Christ without attracting people to Jesus and his church. The good news that Jesus gave us is attractive. Our job is to attract as many people as we can to Jesus and to his church.

There are many things that attract people to a local church: invitations by family and friends; helpful, practical Bible teaching; warm, friendly, positive, and welcoming worship environments; meaningful ministries for children and youth; uplifting and Jesus-exalting music; clean, well-kept facilities. The list could go on. When these things are done and done well, we're doing the work of the church.

The job of the church is to attract. We can't impact until we attract.

- ***Second, the Church Impacts***

  Impact means to have a strong effect on someone or something.

The same kinds of things that positively attract people to church will positively impact them when they attend. People are impacted by the way they are treated, by the order and cleanliness of the facilities, and by the attitudes of the people serving. The location, style, and wording of signs (or absence of them!) impacts, positively or negatively. Small things add up and make a big impact.

Imagine if people pulled into your church parking lot, and the parking team's words or attitudes said, "Don't park there." That would have an impact—a strongly negative one. The same with an usher who said, "Don't sit there." Or a worship team that hasn't practiced recently. Or a sign that said, "Children not allowed." Or a pastor who hasn't studied, prayed, and prepared well. Impact happens in what you do, how you do it, and how you say it.

Impact is not only created by attention to tangible things but to intangible things also. The most important element of impact in the local church is the presence of God. People need to sense that "something is different in this place." And it's more than the decor. It's more than a "cool factor." There needs to be an atmosphere that's permeated with the presence of God. There needs to be a ministry focus that is positive, hope-filled, expecting God to answer prayers, change lives, and speak to people in real ways.

The message of Jesus needs to come through loud and clear, for it's his message that gives hope and transforms hearts. There needs to be an atmosphere that's been spiritually prepared through prayer and sincere worship. Then and only then will people be ready to listen and hear the Word that will change their life direction for eternity.

- ***Third, the Church Assimilates***

  Assimilate: "to assist or cause people to become a part of something"[2]

People who are attracted to church, impacted by the church, and make a decision to give their lives to Jesus Christ need to take the next step. They need to be assimilated into the church family. They need to become a part of the team.

It's wonderful when people's language changes from "that church" to "*my* church"; from, "I go to that church" to "That's *my* church." That's what we mean by assimilation.

It's like getting people who visit your home out of your living room and into your kitchen. If you go to someone's house for the first time, they'll treat you cordially and invite you to sit in the living room and be their guest. The next time, it's less formal. The third time, the china is replaced with regular dishes. The fourth time, it's "Come into the kitchen!" And once they're in the kitchen, in the natural progression, they get involved. They're part of the family. The goal for all who serve in church is to attract people, make sure they're positively impacted when they come, and then help them assimilate—help them become a part of the team.

Research has proven that the best way for people to become a part of church life is through relationships. Once they're involved in a small group or serving, they start developing relationships that help them to get planted in the church. They assimilate. They're now a part of the team.

- ***Fourth, the Church Recuperates***

Recuperate means to heal and recover health and strength.

It's been said that the church is not a museum for saints; it's a hospital for sinners. The church needs ministries that help people recuperate from the destruction and devastation of past sin, bad choices, and painful life experiences.

Many people who come to church are coming from challenging and tough situations. They may be facing a mountain of debt, going through a divorce, dealing with a business failure, or other personal problems. They may be carrying internal pain that has tortured them for decades—guilt, shame, despair. The church is to be a place of solace, comfort, and healing. The atmosphere of the church should be one where people are loved and lifted on their way to life change. This is part of the work Jesus has called us to do. The church needs to be a healing house.

- ***Fifth, the Church Educates***

Educate means to teach and train.

One of the main activities of the church is to teach and train people how to live God's way. Living God's way involves:

- Who we are. Inwardly: in heart and character.
- What we do. Outwardly: in life and witness.

This is called *discipleship*. A healthy church is involved in teaching people how to practically follow Jesus and obey God's Word.

The church has a teaching assignment. Churches are training centers for life. From the cradle to the grave, the church has the opportunity to teach the wisdom and ways of God. We're charged with instructing people in truth that frees them, grows them, matures them, and deploys them in fulfilling service. We've been given the *Word of life!* There's life in God's Word—supernatural power that makes a practical difference in the way people think, feel, and live.

When people are consistently taught God's Word, life is created in them; in their personalities, in their marriages, in their parenting, in their businesses, in their friendships, in their skills and abilities—in every part of their lives. Well-taught people become whole people.

- ***Sixth, the Church Alleviates***

Alleviate: "to make (something) less painful, difficult or severe"[3]

The church is called to alleviate pain and difficulty in the world and in the communities around us. Through outreach and social ministries, the church feeds the hungry, clothes the naked, and helps the disenfranchised—not only with material resources but also with the gospel message that changes lives from the inside out.

It's wonderful when a local church develops a reputation as the go-to place in the community for people in need. While no church can meet all needs, we can meet some needs. While no church can do everything to help all the hurting people around them, they can do something.

These responsibilities go beyond the local community to the world. Every church needs to be doing something significant to reach and help people with the gospel around the world. Through giving and going with strategic global missions, local churches can make a difference thousands of miles away to people they may never meet until heaven. The church's mission is to alleviate pain and poverty—spiritually and otherwise—to the ends of the earth.

- ***Seventh, the Church Replicates***

  Replicate means to reproduce.

The church is called to grow and multiply spiritual fruit. We are called to reproduce disciples, train spiritual leaders, and connect with and pass on faith and church ministry to the next generation. Part of being a disciple involves making other disciples. It's vital to our mission. Together, we're called to replicate and multiply the work of the church and the spiritual workforce of the church.

- ***Eighth, the Church Administrates***

  Administrate means to manage.

Administration is wise planning and managing of ministry resources and activities. Many people don't realize how important administration is to ministry. Actually the root for "administrate" is connected to the root of "ministry." You can't have effective ministry without administration!

The Old Testament character Joseph was not only an amazing leader, he was also an incredible administrator. God gave Egypt seven years of abundant harvests. Joseph didn't waste them. He managed the prosperous times so well so that when the lean times came, people were not without food.

The church needs systems and people who help strategize, organize, and manage ministries. What's managed well generally does well.

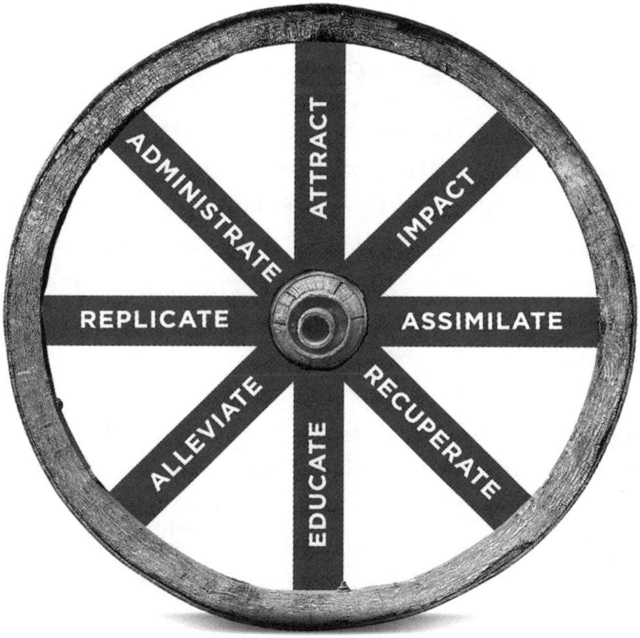

9. Your Significance and Destiny Is Discovered and Fulfilled in the Local Church

Every person is needed and *every* role is important in the church.

I was visiting a church recently and had a conversation with someone working behind the scenes. I asked this individual, "What do you do here at the church?" I can't remember what their particular ministry was, but the person started with, "I just." I didn't hear much of anything after that statement. These words struck me deeply. Think about it. "I just take care of the kids," "I'm just an usher," or "I just park cars." The one word *just* immediately and significantly nullifies the importance of the service.

What I wanted to say to this precious person was, "No, you're a child of God and you're contributing to the work of the Kingdom. You're not 'just' anything. You're a very important part of the body of Christ. There are no nobodies in the body of Christ. Everybody is somebody in the body of Christ. When you bring your gifts you might think they're limited or have no real value. Understand this: *Your gifts have value to God!* You're important!"

When we get to heaven, I think we'll all be surprised at how Jesus measures things. The "first shall be last; and the last shall be first" (Mathew 19:30 KJV). Never think of yourself as "just" anything. You are a significant part of the body of Christ. Look at the way Paul described the importance of every person in the church:

> There are different kinds of gifts, but the same Spirit distributes them. There are different kinds of service, but the same Lord. There are different kinds of

> working, but in all of them and in everyone it is the same God at work. Now to each one the manifestation of the Spirit is given for the common good ... Just as a body, though one, has many parts, but all its many parts form one body, so it is with Christ. For we were all baptized by one Spirit so as to form one body—whether Jews or Gentiles, slave or free—and we were all given the one Spirit to drink. Even so, the body is not made up of one part but of many ... Now you are the body of Christ, and each one of you is a part of it. (1 Corinthians 12:4-7, 12-14, 27 NIV)

10. God Sees Those Who Serve in His Church and Promises Eternal Rewards to Those Who Faithfully Do Their Part

Many people who serve in the church work long hours during the week. They carry the pressure of their careers. They face the stress of a daily commute. They feel the demands of finances, the challenges of living life in a fast-paced world, the issues of family life, and a host of other things. Yet, after their hours at work and home responsibilities, they show up and serve God's people. God sees and appreciates this. God will reward this. That's how God builds his church—with people like this. These labors are noted in God's book in heaven. God records every effort and sacrifice made for his Kingdom and church.

Look at the reward that awaits people like this:

> His master replied, "Well done, good and faithful servant! You have been faithful with a few things; I will

> put you in charge of many things. Come and share your master's happiness!" (Matthew 25:21 NIV)

When Paul looked at the end of his life, wrapping things up, knowing he was soon going to die, he wrote:

> For I am already being poured out like a drink offering, and the time for my departure is near. I have fought the good fight, I have finished the race, I have kept the faith. Now there is in store for me the crown of righteousness, which the Lord, the righteous Judge, will award to me on that day—and not only to me, but also to all who have longed for his appearing. (2 Timothy 4:6-8 NIV)

Think about that. You get to heaven and Jesus basically says, "I saw everything you did for me. I saw your faithfulness, and now I have something for you."

Think about what it would be like to be recognized for some work you did by a world-renowned leader or someone you highly esteemed. How much more rewarding will it be when the Lord of the universe says, "My child, I want to honor you. Here's a crown of righteousness for your service to me. You fought the good fight. You finished the race with faithfulness. Now, here's a reward for you." It's exhilarating to think about, isn't it?

The sixteenth chapter of the book of Romans is Paul's remembrance of many different people who helped him in his ministry. Paul thanked this person, that person, this woman who was like a mother to him, that person who was like a sister, these people who were so valuable in his life. He lists lots of people who made it possible for him to do what he did. This is the great apostle Paul writing these words. He was amazing. He wrote most of the New Testament. What a phenomenal man he was. Yet he said publicly, for all of us in all ages to know, "I couldn't have done it without this team." If Paul remembered the work of others, how much more will God remember and reward those who serve him!

Everyone is important in Jesus' church. That means you! And your faithful service to Jesus and his church will be rewarded. He watches and records your investment in his work.

God has a dream—to build his church in the earth, and he wants you on his team. It's the most exciting and rewarding investment you'll ever make in your life.

In the next few chapters, we'll look at the key decisions that will help you become an incredible part of God's dream team!

Power Points

Ten Things You Need to Know about the Church

1. The church is all believers everywhere who know Jesus Christ as Savior and Lord.

2. You can't separate Jesus from his church.

3. Local churches are key to God's plan for reaching the world.
4. To love Jesus, we must also love what Jesus loves, and Jesus loves his church.
5. To flourish, we need to be planted in a local church.
6. The church has a mission to fulfill that can't be fulfilled without workers.
7. The fulfillment of the church's mission requires a positive, Kingdom-minded culture.
8. The fulfillment of the church's mission requires strong, systematic activities and ministries.
9. Your significance and destiny are discovered and fulfilled in the local church.
10. God sees those who serve in his church and promises eternal rewards to those who faithfully fulfill their part in it.

Eight Things an Effective Church Must Do Well

1. Attract
2. Impact
3. Assimilate
4. Recuperate
5. Educate
6. Alleviate
7. Replicate
8. Administrate

Power Prayer

Father, thank you for your love.

Thank you for the church.

I pray for my church today.

Use it to reach people with the gospel of Jesus Christ.

Use my church to fulfill your dream that none should perish but that all should come to the knowledge of the truth.

Help me be faithful in the task, and fill me with the Holy Spirit as I serve you and love others.

Thank you for it, in Jesus' name. Amen.

Chapter 2

Develop Your Character

Serving Others Starts with the "Law of Depth"

My home water supply comes from a well. Occasionally we have to monitor the water quality. I've learned that the quality of water in a well is determined by its depth. If a well is shallow, you run the risk of groundwater contamination. Water from a shallow well can be deadly. Deep is better. When depth is present, something strong and healthy can be built. Depth provides safety. Depth protects from pollution.

But depth costs something to achieve.

In the construction world, lots of money is spent on the parts of a structure that are never seen but are essential to its endurance. If investment in a solid foundation is shortchanged, it will eventually become evident.

The Washington Monument has always intrigued me because it's one of the most visible landmarks in Washington, DC. From many parts of the city, you see its profile towering above the landscape. How has it stood the test of time? How has it been able to endure?

In 1791, two years into George Washington's first term as president, a place to memorialize him was envisioned by Pierre L'Enfant. L'Enfant designed the layout of Washington, DC, with a prominent space reserved to honor its premier leader. In 1845, a design was drawn up for an obelisk to stand in that space. Construction began in 1848. When it was completed in 1884, the Monument was 555 feet tall—making it the tallest building in the world at the time. Without all the advances in engineering we have today, how is something envisioned in the 1700s and built in the

1800s still standing? What holds it up? The answer is found in the foundation—a massive support structure, thirty-seven feet deep and fifty-five feet wide. The Washington Monument has survived because it has substance beneath it.

The point is, the height of a building is always determined by the quality and depth of its foundation. You can't go high without first going deep.

Have you ever seen a building that's sinking? First, the cracks give it away. They tell you that something is happening you can't fully see ... yet. These outward signs warn you of a more serious issue. It's only a matter of time before the little cracks reveal a significant and potentially dangerous underlying problem.

In Shanghai, China, a group of real estate and construction personnel were thrown in prison when an apartment building fell in 2009, killing one person. It didn't collapse, but tipped over. Fortunately, it landed short of neighboring buildings, so there wasn't a massive disaster or collateral damage. What was the problem? They cheated on the building's foundation.

A number of years ago, as I watched the construction of our main church campus facility, I was amazed at how long it took to put in the foundation. I was on the site when the concrete trucks rolled in to pour the footers. I was shocked! I couldn't believe how much material and money was required for this phase of the project.

I actually thought, "How much concrete could you possibly need for a foundation?" As this unending line of trucks continued rolling in, I felt like saying, "Hey, let's see if we can get by with just a little less concrete!" Now I'm so glad the builders knew what they were doing. The building is still standing and shows no signs of falling apart, despite its constant use.

I'm reminded of two things when I reflect on that experience:

First, I took no pictures of the foundation. The footings didn't seem photo-worthy. At no time since then has anyone driven up to our building and said, "Wow, that's a beautiful foundation! Can I see a portrait of the footers?" Foundations aren't beautiful, but they *are* essential.

Second, it costs something to build a foundation. It isn't built without a significant investment.

The Law of Depth states that depth determines height and durability. It's true in construction and in life. The consequences of a shallow life, shallow commitments, shallow relationships, or a shallow approach to ministry eventually show up.

Even in church life, shallowness will eventually come to light in a person and in their ministry assignments. You cannot fool the Law of Depth! For the church to be effective, we must accept responsibility to develop both spiritual and character depth. You can't fake it. You can't cover up for its lack.

Depth is something that requires effort and investment. It involves inside, "underground," personal work that others generally never see. While character-building effort is unseen, the fruit *is* seen.

Foundation work is always worth the investment.

Why? Because among many other things, depth makes us usable by God.

Unfortunately, we humans are often more interested in and impressed by the *seen* talent of a person than their *unseen* character. Scripture reminds us of this natural tendency: "People look on the outward appearance, but the Lord looks on the heart" (1 Samuel 16:7 NIV). It's true. All of us tend to look at exteriors. As a result, people easily substitute and celebrate the superficial over the substantial. We're quick to be wowed by the gifts we see in a person without taking time to consider spiritual and character depth. We forget that, like a tall building without a good foundation, giftedness without character depth is an accident waiting to happen.

Character Is the Foundation for Ministry.
Gifts Are the Expressions of Ministry.

Serving in church involves using our talents for the glory of God and the good of the church. Your gifts are how ministry comes through you. Depth of character is what enables your gifts to be used and sustained over the long haul. It's the foundation for your gifts.

Gifts are *given*, but character is *formed*. You don't *choose* or *earn* your basic gifts and talents. Your gifts are freely given to you by God. Look at what the Bible says:

> For God's gifts and his call are irrevocable.
> (Romans 11:29 NIV)

> Every good and perfect gift is from above, coming down from the Father of the heavenly lights, who does not change like shifting shadows. (James 1:17 NIV)
>
> He said: "A man of noble birth went to a distant country to have himself appointed king and then to return. So he called ten of his servants and gave them ten minas. 'Put this money to work,' he said, 'until I come back.'" (Luke 19:12, 13 NIV)
>
> There are different kinds of spiritual gifts, but the same Spirit is the source of them all. There are different kinds of service, but we serve the same Lord. God works in different ways, but it is the same God who does the work in all of us. A spiritual gift is given to each of us so we can help each other. (1 Corinthians 12:4-7 NLT)
>
> Each of you should use whatever gift you have received to serve others, as faithful stewards of God's grace in its various forms. (1 Peter 4:10 NIV)

As a uniquely created person, you have something special to add to the life and ministry of the church. God expects you to use the gifts he gave you in the work of his Kingdom. The contribution of your gifts, in connection and harmony with the gifts of others, results in a beautiful symphony that honors God and blesses people. All of us working together make a church. Each one of us is vitally important to God. But our gifts need to be solidly secured on the foundation of deep character.

Five Essential Facts about Spiritual Gifts

Before we dive into the issue of character more fully, let's take a few minutes and focus more specifically on spiritual gifts. It's an often misunderstood concept.

Dedicating and contributing your gifts to God and his church are important parts of your spiritual growth and your usefulness to God. But like anything else, you can't use something well or wisely without first understanding some basic things about it. This is true for spiritual gifts. There are at least five things you need to know about your gifts.

1. Gifts Are Neither Self-Determined nor Self-Confirmed

You don't determine your own gifts. God determines them. Neither do you confirm your own gifts. They are confirmed by the people around you, in relationship with you.

We've all seen people in television contests who think they can sing, but who actually can't sing at all. They're self-deceived. They're *absolutely sure* they're going to win an album deal. Their problem is that they haven't submitted themselves to the wisdom and observations of others. If they had, they might have received the feedback they needed to choose a different path—and spare our ears.

In the same way, you and I have spiritual gifts that can and should be confirmed by the people around us. You might think you can sing, but if people don't enjoy listening to you, you can't sing. You might think you can preach, but if people don't want to hear you, you're not a communicator. Whatever you think your gifts are, they need to be observed, affirmed, and confirmed by trusted, mature people in your life. We're not talking about becoming a slave to other's opinions. We're talking about a reality check. If your gift is real, it will be evident to others.

2. The Growth of Your Gifts Requires Training

Gifts come in raw form. They need to be developed, polished, and refined. This requires an investment on your part. You also have to let others help you. Other people play a major role in helping you discover and grow your gifts. This means that for your gifts to grow into usable form, you need to be teachable, trainable, and responsive to help and input from others.

3. Your Gifts Don't Make You a Superstar or Grant You Special Exceptions

Some gifted people earn an unwanted title called "diva." Their attitude is, "I've got this gift—don't touch me! Pamper me! Coddle me! Let me do everything my way!"

God's gifts never make you a superstar, and certainly shouldn't make you a diva. The greatest and most effective servants of God get this:

- Gifts are not meant to build you up; gifts are meant to build up the church.
- Gifts are not meant to give you a platform. They're meant to advance the church and the ministries of the church—to strengthen the platform of the church.

Your gifts are never about you. Remember, your gifts are never about platforming, promoting, or posturing yourself for popularity or promotion. They never give you special exceptions morally or ethically. They don't entitle you to certain privileges. They're to be used for the good and growth of God's church and Kingdom, and for the glory of God.

4. Giftedness Is Never a Reason for Pride

While some are highly enamored with their own gifts, others are unsure if they even have any. *You do*. You are gifted by God. Review the previous Scriptures about spiritual gifts. These verses are meant for you. Each of these passages reminds us that gifts are given and that these gifts come from God. You are gifted, for sure!

Did you *earn* your gifts and talents? No. You didn't do a single thing to get the gift package God gave you. To boast about your gifts is to take credit for something that you have no right to claim credit for. Everyone has gifts, and every gift we have *comes* from God and *belongs* to God. Instead of making you arrogant, your gifts should humble you and make you deeply appreciative to such a good and generous God.

5. You Can Discover Your Spiritual Gifts

If you haven't discovered your gifts, here are three simple steps that will guide you to finding them.

- ***Step 1: Have a "Where Can I Help?" Mentality***

This is where it all starts. Be available! It's been said that availability is more important than ability to God. He can give you ability, but he will not force your availability. You choose to make yourself available to be used by him. How? Have an attitude that says:

- How can I help?
- How can I be a part of the life of this church?
- Does anything need to be done?
- I'm ready to help.

This attitude of availability is what gets you started.

- ***Step 2: Realize That Over Time You Will Be Attracted to Specific Areas of Ministry and Will Blossom in Them***

Over time, your ministry passions will surface and fruit will be evident. As you faithfully serve wherever needed, you will discover your *sweet spot* of ministry.

Some people who start in the nursery ministry quickly discover that crying babies aren't their passion. Nevertheless, they were available. They may eventually move on to another ministry in the church, but their availability to serve got them started. Some people may go through several ministries before they find the spot that brings out the "Wow!" in them. The key is to get started somewhere.

God will direct you, but he won't push you. As you start moving, he gives you direction. Evangelist Reinhard Bonnke often says, "God goes with the goers, he doesn't sit with the sitters." It's easier to steer a moving car than a parked car. So just sign up somewhere and serve with all your might, whatever the need may be.

When you start serving, God will move you toward the discovery of your gift. When you feel passionate about serving in an area and fruit is seen in what you're doing, your heart will say (and people around you will affirm), "This is *my* place!"

- ***Step 3: Be Sensitive to the Feedback, Training, and Guidance of Spiritual Leaders and Mature Christians***

God will use his people, especially your spiritual leaders, to affirm and confirm your gifts.

If you're a greeter but you have a disagreeable personality, at some point, someone will likely, and maybe kindly say, "We need to work on your personality or find a different place for you!" In situations like these, either God is using the position to highlight something he wants to address in your life or it's possible that the position is not the best place for you. The people appointed to guide you can then help you find a ministry that better suits your gifts, skills, and personality.

Remember that gifts are just gifts. Don't be super impressed with your or someone else's gifts. Very gifted people are often popular and celebrated, but what really matters is what's inside—whether their gifts rest on solid character. Character is the foundation for a successful life and effective ministry.

Through the years, many gifted people have wreaked havoc in the spiritual lives of others and brought disgrace and division to the body of Christ because of weak, flawed, or even twisted character. This happens because gifted people are frequently given too many ministry opportunities and too much ministry responsibility without first proving their character.

Your character is the heart out of which you do everything you do. Your present and future success are determined by it. It also determines the legacy you will leave beyond this life, and the eternal rewards you receive in heaven as a believer in Jesus Christ. Your gifts will not impress God in heaven because they were meant to be used on earth. But you will take to heaven your character.

Character Is about Quality

The Greek word *dokimé*, often translated as "character" in the New Testament, means "proof of genuineness, trustworthiness; the fact that one has proven oneself true or the act of proving oneself true."[4]

In the days when the New Testament was written, *dokimé* was regularly used to describe metals that had been tested and shown to be authentic. It was associated with the mark of quality. The root of the word deals with metals and signifies a proving process. Lawrence Richards, a biblical word scholar, states, "The word [character] … draws our attention to testing as a means of determining genuineness and thus as a grounds for giving approval."[5]

With fine jewelry, sterling tableware or expensive knives, you'll find a stamp on the metal. That stamp is its proof of authenticity or *dokimé*. It authenticates that the metal is what it purports to be.

- If you buy a diamond, you get a certificate of authenticity that proves it is what it says it is.
- If you look at a gold bracelet, you'll see it marked 10 karats, 14 karats, 18 karats, or even 24 karats. The mark tells you that it's been tested and verified to be what it claims to be.

The same is true about character.

What is required for gold to move from 10 karats to 24 karats? Purity! It's the same with us. As we purify our character, God marks us as useful, valuable, prepared for greater service.

How are we purified? God tests us, checks us out, watches how we respond to situations, monitors the attitudes of our hearts. He pays attention to how faithfully we serve him, and how joyously we obey him. These processes help cleanse us internally and make us ready for all God has for us.

The good news is that we can all become 24-karat believers. Wherever you are today doesn't define where you can end up, if you choose to grow.

Purity produces quality. Most of us appreciate quality when we see or experience it. We're willing to invest more in something that has it.

Quality is all about:

- The process used to make something.
- The material used in making it.
- The lasting ability it possesses.
- The testimony of qualified people who have tested or used it.

People of character are well put together. They have inward integrity. People of character rise to the top, no matter what situation they find themselves in.

Remember the Old Testament character Joseph? He was sold into slavery by his brothers to a prominent Egyptian named Potiphar. Before long, he was running Potiphar's palace. After being falsely accused of rape, Joseph was thrown in prison. What happened? He was soon running the prison. Eventually, he went from being a prison trustee to prime minister of Egypt. Why? Because Joseph had character!

Joseph's character shines again when his brothers, the ones who hated him and betrayed him, came to Egypt in search of food in a time of famine. Joseph fed them and forgave them. His depth of character was amazing.

This is what character looks like. People with it demonstrate spiritual depth, moral strength, godly wisdom, graceful actions and attitudes, mature thinking, responsible living, faithful commitments, and sound decision making.

The apostle Paul understood the value of character in those who worked with him in ministry. A young man named John Mark was part of Paul's first church-planting trip. John Mark bailed out on his first ministry assignment because he had not yet developed the inner qualities necessary for ministry. His lack of character showed up under pressure. Paul would not allow John Mark to be on his team until some character issues were addressed.

John Mark was the first person fired from a ministry team. He wasn't fired because of an outward moral failure. He was sent home because he was complaining. He was upset because life and ministry were hard. Paul temporarily disqualified a young man from ministry because he lacked the inner maturity needed for the calling. Later, John Mark's character developed and as a result, we now have the gospel of Mark, written by him.

On the other hand, Paul highly valued another young man in ministry because of the character he demonstrated. His name was Timothy. Take a look at Paul's admiration for the depth of character Timothy possessed:

> But I trust in the Lord Jesus to send Timothy to you shortly, that I also may be encouraged when I know your state. For I have no one like-minded, who will sincerely care for your state. For all seek their own, not the things which are of Christ Jesus. But you know his proven character, that as a son with *his* father he served with me in the gospel. (Philippians 2:19-22 NKJV)

Timothy became an indispensable and well-respected aide to Paul because he was a quality man. He had the inner qualities that stood the test of time and pressure—even as a young man (1 Timothy 4:12).

Character is all about quality.

When you buy gold, you want to know that it's real gold. When you serve God and his church, you want to make sure you're developing the character qualities God approves.

Character Must Be Developed

Gifts are given; character is *developed.*

How do we develop the kind of character that will stand the test of time and bring honor to God? While God works in and around us to deepen our character, our responses to him are critical. God's work in us is never completed without us doing our part. We must cooperate with the process. We must proactively take key steps in this journey.

How to Develop Deeper Character

Here are some practical things you can do to develop your character. Let's look at four proactive steps you can take to become the person God wants you to be.

1. Be Aware of Your Character Issues

We're all affected by sin and sinful influences. Given the best family backgrounds and the most positive life experiences and personal choices, our character still has gaping holes and serious structural defects, all because of sin. Our eyes need to be opened to the sinful areas that continue to linger in our soul so they can be addressed.

What is one of the best prayers you'll ever pray? "God show me the real 'me.'" It's a courageous and extremely important prayer. When you pray this way, God will show you things about yourself you've never seen before. And usually, it's ugly and painful at first sight. But this is how you grow. These moments of self-awareness can become defining moments for you if you will seek them and learn from them.

Why is this prayer so important? Because you can't work on issues if you don't know they're there. To be who you need to be you must first see what you need to see! It's only when you see the real you that you are able to get to work on your real issues.

The psalmist David grew his character by praying this way:

> Search me, God, and know my heart; test me and know my anxious thoughts. See if there is any offensive way in me, and lead me in the way everlasting. (Psalm 139:23, 24 NIV)

Be courageous and pray this prayer. It's a way to grow your character.

2. Uncover the Roots of Your Character Issues

Many of our character problems are rooted in baggage from the past. Character issues are often connected to unresolved hurts, soul pain, resentment, bitterness, disappointments, and regrets. Character can be weakened and twisted by how we've reacted to, and the way we think about, past events and situations.

We often develop sinful and dysfunctional ways of handling soul pain from our yesterdays. These unholy and unhealthy coping mechanisms can become our mental, emotional, and relational *modus operandi*—our way of doing things. To experience real character change, it's important for these root issues and patterns to be uncovered, confronted, and converted to holy and healthy ways of thinking and living by God's grace.

Let's say that you grew up in an abusive family and you developed a deep hatred for your mom or dad. You then went into adulthood with this poison buried inside you. Even though you may not realize it, this ugly stuff in your soul will continue to affect who you are and what you do. This suppressed resentment will twist your character. It will change the way you look at people, how you interact with people, your trust of others, and a whole host of other things in your life. The painful things you experienced but haven't processed well will continue to haunt and control you. They weigh you down and work against you.

To experience character change, it's important for these root issues to be uncovered, confronted, and dealt with by God's love and grace. Don't let bitter roots from your yesterdays rob you of the life God has for you today.

Take a look at some Bible verses that encourage us to address and move past our past:

> Not that I have already obtained all this, or have already arrived at my goal, but I press on to take hold of that for which Christ Jesus took hold of me. Brothers and sisters, I do not consider myself yet to have taken hold of it. But one thing I do: Forgetting what is behind and straining toward what is ahead, I press on toward

> the goal to win the prize for which God has called me heavenward in Christ Jesus. (Philippians 3:12-14 NIV)
>
> See to it that no one falls short of the grace of God and that no bitter root grows up to cause trouble and defile many. (Hebrews 12:15 NIV)

3. Practice the Activities That Welcome God's Grace and Power into Your Life

Character growth only happens when we make room for God to work in us. God works in people who open doors for him by practicing certain spiritual disciplines. Practices like consistent Bible study, meditation on Scripture, prayer, fasting, and church participation position us to receive God's grace and the power to change.

Remember:

- **The Word of God is powerful.**

It washes us, heals us, and delivers us. Take time each day to read and think about God's Word. It may be as little as five or ten minutes a day, but as you do, something incredible happens inside you. God changes you for the better as you saturate yourself with his Word.

- **Prayer works.**

Spend time each day in prayer. Prayer is simply opening your heart to God, and listening for his response. Make this a daily habit. It welcomes the presence of God and allows him to work in and around you.

- **Worship and study with other believers in church changes you.**

Be consistent in your church attendance. Actively participate in worship. Eagerly receive the teaching of God's Word. Apply what you learn. These practices make a major difference in your life.

Here are a few verses that underscore the power of these activities:

> Keep this Book of the Law always on your lips; meditate on it day and night, so that you may be careful to do everything written in it. Then you will be prosperous and successful. (Joshua 1:8 NIV)
>
> The unfolding of your words gives light; it gives understanding to the simple. (Psalm 119:130 NIV)
>
> So He said to them, "This kind can come out by nothing but prayer and fasting." (Mark 9:29 NKJV)
>
> Physical training is good, but training for godliness is much better, promising benefits in this life and in the life to come. (1 Timothy 4:8 NLT)

4. Seek the Help of Others

God uses other people to assist you in the development of your character. People around you can help you see character issues in your life that you may not see yourself. Having trusted, mature advisers and mentors in your life that can help you improve your character is key to becoming the person God wants you to be.

One of the first and best places to grow your character is at home. My wife tells me the truth about me—sometimes straight up! Marriage is "*brutiful*," isn't it? My wife isn't impressed with my title. She knows the real me and is able to help me grow. She's courageous enough to speak truth into my life, and I'm glad. It makes me better.

Develop eyes and ears that are quick to learn from others. I've learned so much over the years through the people in our church, and through others God has brought into my life. Even the tough, painful things we experience in relationships can transform us for good if we handle them the right way.

Instead of blaming others, rationalizing our bad attitudes, and justifying our graceless reactions when someone hurts or disappoints you, look into the mirror at yourself. What's the situation teaching you about you? What do you need to learn? Instead of seeing the speck in someone else's eye, reflect on the "log that's in your own eye" (Matthew 7:3-5 ESV).

The Bible says:

> Two are better than one, because they have a good return for their labor. (Ecclesiastes 4:9 NIV)
>
> As iron sharpens iron, so one person sharpens another. (Proverbs 27:17 NIV)

To be a part of God's dream team, and to attract others to be a part, we must, with determination and dedication, choose to develop our character. That deep character will produce a strong life and a strong ministry.

Power Points

- Serving others starts with the "Law of Depth."
- Character is the foundation for ministry. Gifts are the expressions of ministry.
- There are five essential facts about spiritual gifts.
- Character is about quality.
- Character must be developed.

Power Prayer

Father, show me what's going on in me.
Reveal to me character issues in my life
so I can see them and grow,
in the name of Jesus, Amen.

Chapter 3

Be Responsible

Partners. Who do you think of when you see this word? Perhaps Larry Page and Sergey Brin? Or Bill Gates and Paul Allen? Or maybe Steve Jobs and Steve Wozniak? Maybe you think of McCartney and Lennon, Ricky and Lucy, or Batman and Robin. If you've flown recently, maybe you think of the Wright brothers.

A historic collaboration I find fascinating is the friendship between Thomas Edison and Henry Ford. Ford once worked for Edison but left to develop the automobile, with Edison's encouragement. When they reunited, Ford—the maverick millionaire—idolized Edison, the brilliant, and often cash-strapped, inventor. They helped each other, alternately inspiring and looking out for the other.

Their summer automobile camping trips—complete with a kitchen car that supplied a formal dining tent—became so famous, the men even hosted a US president. The two shared recreation, brilliant conversation, and other mutual friendships such as with Harvey Firestone. Eventually, they partnered on a research project, building side-by-side residences in Fort Myers, Florida, where they planted extensive gardens and built a lab to work on experiments with rubber.

Their mutual esteem and respect never diminished. When Edison died, his son carried out his father's wishes, giving Ford a sealed test tube that contained Edison's final breath. The tube is still on display at the Henry Ford Museum.

Whether or not we've ever experienced such a close friendship, collaboration, or partnership as these men did, we've entered into an even more intimate and important partnership. God has called us into a partnership with *him*. Partnering with God, the Creator of the universe, demands a level of responsibility that has to be learned and cultivated.

Partnership with God Requires Accepting Responsibility

You can't understand partnership without also understanding the concept of responsibility.

The biblical principle of responsibility is critical to serving God and others. Think of parenting. The goal of parenting is not to get your kids out of the house, but to prepare them to be good citizens, valuable workers, and wise parents themselves some day. A big part of growing up involves the awareness and acceptance of responsibility. You could say the real goal of raising children is to produce responsible adults.

Accepting responsibility is a personal choice that's necessary for success in all areas of life. Successful marriages and families along with successful institutions and organizations are all built by people who have learned to be responsible and to bear responsibility.

You can look at the history of any major institution—universities, hospitals, churches—and you'll find people who bore the weight of founding, leading, and managing it. Institutions don't survive—let alone thrive—without responsible people shouldering the burden and moving them forward, responsibly.

This principle is also true for the local church. Remember, while the church is a living, breathing *organism*, empowered by the Holy Spirit, it is also an *organization* that has a job to do in the world. Church is not simply a gathering place, it's a place where people get things done for the Kingdom of God—they advance the gospel in the world. The church is a living, breathing organism empowered by the Holy Spirit, *and* an organization that has a mission to fulfill.

The fulfillment of this mission and the success of this work happen as believers in Jesus partner responsibly with God in his work.

It's amazing to think about: God chooses us as his partners in the mission and work of his church and the advance of his Kingdom in the world! God takes folks like you and me and brings us into his "family business." He invites us to be a real part of *his* enterprise.

What a privilege—and a responsibility.

In partnerships, each person has a part. What would Steve Jobs have been without Steve Wozniak? A successful business partnership happens only when partners do their part. A happy marriage happens only when both spouses accept their responsibilities. A business partnership only succeeds when partners are fully engaged. Winning teams happen when every team member brings their best.

What the Bible Says about Partnership with God

The Bible is clear about our partnership with God:

> We are God's coworkers. You are God's field. You are God's building. (1 Corinthians 3:9 GW)

> As God's partners, we beg you not to accept this marvelous gift of God's kindness and then ignore it. (2 Corinthians 6:1 NLT)

> For we are God's handiwork, created in Christ Jesus to do good works, which God prepared in advance for us to do. (Ephesians 2:10 NIV)

> But how can they call on him to save them unless they believe in him? And how can they believe in him if they have never heard about him? And how can they hear about him unless someone tells them? And how will anyone go and tell them without being sent? That is why the Scriptures say, "How beautiful are the feet of messengers who bring good news!" (Romans 10:14, 15 NLT)

While God is ultimately responsible for building his church, he's brought us in on the process. Every believer in Jesus is called to work with God in a responsible way to assist in this mission. While God enables and empowers us by his Spirit to do his work, he expects us to use the spiritual resources and natural gifting he provides to work together with him. The apostle Paul said it this way:

> So Christ himself gave the apostles, the prophets, the evangelists, the pastors and teachers, to equip his people for works of service, so that the body of Christ may be built up until we all reach unity in the faith and in the knowledge of the Son of God and become mature, attaining to the whole measure of the fullness of Christ. Then we will no longer be infants, tossed back and forth by the waves, and blown here and there by every wind of teaching and by the cunning and craftiness of people in their deceitful scheming. Instead, speaking the truth in love, we will grow to become in every respect the mature body of him who is the head, that is, Christ. From him the whole body, joined and held together by every supporting ligament, grows and builds itself up in love, as each part does its work. (Ephesians 4:11-16 NIV)

Paul is saying that *everybody* has a part to play in the building of Jesus' church.

This should convince you of how important you are to God. So many people think pastors do all the ministry work. Absolutely not! I certainly believe in hard-working pastors. But strong, life-giving, life-changing churches are built by partners working together with pastors and spiritual leaders, and most importantly with God, to get the job done.

Five Characteristics of a Responsible Person

The church is only as strong as its people. An irresponsible person will never build a great life. Irresponsible believers will never build a great church. Great churches are built by people who take their spiritual responsibilities seriously.

Let's take a look at some of the characteristics of a responsible person.

1. Responsible People Commit

Commitment simply means to make something a priority and because of that, you exclude other things. To say, "I'm committed to my spouse," means that I make my spouse a priority and exclude other things that may conflict with or undermine my marriage relationship. If I'm committed to my Bible study, I have to exclude other things that would conflict with it. In other words, commitment involves both inclusion and exclusion.

Responsibility begins with commitment. You'll never accept responsibility for something until you're committed to it.

This is true in the personal arena of life. Performing well academically, athletically, professionally, and spiritually starts with commitment. Commitment is what takes you forward when others stay behind. Commitment is what causes you to get things done when others are fantasizing, procrastinating, or making excuses. Good intentions don't count unless you add commitment to them. Responsible people make and keep commitments.

Commitment is the glue that holds you in relationships so that you can grow. Sometimes relationships get tough and you want to run. What keeps you in a relationship is commitment.

Commitment is the foundation for spiritual growth. To grow spiritually, you must be *all in* with God, and *all in* with the church where he's planted you. You must say, "God is my God, Jesus Christ is my Lord, and this is the community of believers I am called to. I will live the Jesus-life here, and do Jesus' work here. I'm committed!"

The ministry of Jesus is all about calling people to accept their responsibility to commit:

> As Jesus was walking beside the Sea of Galilee, he saw two brothers, Simon called Peter and his brother Andrew. They were casting a net into the lake, for they were fishermen. "Come, follow me," Jesus said, "and I will send you out to fish for people." At once they left their nets and followed him. Going on from there, he saw two other brothers, James son of Zebedee and his brother John. They were in a boat with their father Zebedee, preparing their nets. Jesus called them, and immediately they left the boat and their father and followed him. (Matthew 4:18-22 NIV)

Jesus called these men to make a commitment. He said, "Come follow me and I will make you fishers of men." Their whole future hinged on their response in that moment. They couldn't become the people God wanted them to be unless they left their boats behind, gave up their old life and said, "I'm going with you, Jesus."

In that moment, their commitment positioned them to eventually become apostles and early church leaders. The future, unbeknownst to them, turned on that one choice that set them toward their destiny. Jesus extends the same call to commitment to us:

> Then he said to them all: "Whoever wants to be my disciple must deny themselves and take up their cross daily and follow me. For whoever wants to save their life will lose it, but whoever loses their life for me will save it. What good is it for someone to gain the whole world, and yet lose or forfeit their very self? Whoever is ashamed of me and my words, the Son of Man will be ashamed of them when he comes in his glory and in the glory of the Father and of the holy angels." (Luke 9:23-26 NIV)

> In the same way, those of you who do not give up everything you have cannot be my disciples. (Luke 14:33 NIV)

> They devoted themselves to the apostles' teaching and to fellowship, to the breaking of bread and to prayer. (Acts 2:42 NIV)

> But whatever were gains to me I now consider loss for the sake of Christ. What is more, I consider everything a loss because of the surpassing worth

> of knowing Christ Jesus my Lord, for whose sake I have lost all things. I consider them garbage, that I may gain Christ. (Philippians 3:7, 8 NIV)

True commitment is a long-term acceptance of responsibility. Commitment says:

- I'm not giving up.
- I'm not quitting.
- I'm going to fulfill what I said I would do, no matter what comes my way or what I feel at any moment.
- You can count on me for the long haul.

Responsible people commit!

2. Responsible People Connect

Part of commitment is connection. When you commit your life to Jesus, you begin a life journey of connecting with God. When you commit yourself to the community, mission, and work of his church, you begin an ongoing journey of connecting with other people.

It's impossible to genuinely connect with God and refuse to connect with his people. The Bible principle is clear:

Loving God = Loving People

They go together. The cross is both vertical and horizontal. The work of the cross is to reconcile us to God and to reconcile us to one another.

Jesus died to save us from anything that would keep us from a meaningful and personal relationship with God, and from positive and impacting relationships with other people.

This work of reconciling people to one another is clearly seen in the first-century church. During that time in church history, the biggest thing that kept believers apart was the cultural conflict between Jews and Gentiles. Their perspectives were different. Their backgrounds were different. Their attitudes about life were different. Basically, the only thing they held in common was faith in Jesus Christ.

One of the triumphs of the early church was the miracle of mixed cultures worshiping together in unity and harmony. The early church brought together people with Jewish, Gentile, heathen, and pagan backgrounds to worship and service under the banner of Jesus Christ. Their new identity was *Christian*!

Still today, the church is made up of people from different cultures and backgrounds. We're called to come together under the authority of Jesus Christ, connecting with God and connecting with one another. Because of what Jesus did on the cross and in his resurrection, people from every nation, race, tribe, and tongue become one family, worshiping one Savior, in unity and harmony. Our new identity is *Christian.*

Responsible people understand that they need to be a part of something bigger than themselves. They realize that the enlargement of their lives will be affected by who, where, and to what they connect. Responsible people don't live in isolation. Our lives have their fullest meaning in community.

My own life is bigger and better because of my connection with people in our church. The variety of cultures, generations, and backgrounds of people in our church family enhances my life. It's taught me many wonderful things. I can't imagine what my life would be like if I hadn't learned the value of connecting with other believers.

Serving in church is more than doing a job. It's about building relationships with the people you serve and those who serve with you. Ministry is not some isolated, insulated action. It's a people connection. Wonderful things happen when we say: "I will be vulnerable, share my life with others, and open up to the people around me. I will let other people open up to me. I will help carry their burdens, and allow them to help me carry my burdens. We're part of each other's lives." That's what community is. That's what church is.

Responsible people become a part of a community that lives and serves together for a unified purpose. Strong community life requires meaningful connections that come as people open themselves to others, pray with others, and work alongside others for a common goal. Part of your responsibility is to value and prayerfully pursue these connections.

Together, we become a part of something bigger than ourselves or the part we play. We play different parts, but we're all on the same team.

The "us" of church life is in the Bible from the very beginning:

> "Let us make mankind in our image, in our likeness, so that they may rule over the fish in the sea...." (Genesis 1:26 NIV)

Note the "us" and "our." God is One, yet he exists in the context of community himself. There's unity in the Trinity.

God then proceeded to describe the importance of human relationships. He defined the reason we're made in his image, "so that *they* may rule over the fish…." Note the plural pronoun "they." It's a relationship word. It wasn't "him" or "her," it was "they." Everything God does, he does in the context of relationships and community.

Look at God's emphasis on connection:

> Two are better than one, because they have a good return for their labor: If either of them falls down, one can help the other up. But pity anyone who falls and has no one to help them up. Also, if two lie down together, they will keep warm. But how can one keep warm alone? Though one may be overpowered, two can defend themselves. A cord of three strands is not quickly broken. (Ecclesiastes 4:9-12 NIV)

> They devoted themselves to the apostles' teaching and to fellowship, to the breaking of bread and to prayer. Everyone was filled with awe at the many wonders and signs performed by the apostles. All the believers were together and had everything in common. They sold property and possessions to give to anyone who had need. Every day they continued to meet together in the temple courts. They broke bread in their homes and ate together with glad and sincere hearts, praising God and enjoying the favor of all the

> people. And the Lord added to their number daily those who were being saved. (Acts 2:42-47 NIV)
>
> Not giving up meeting together, as some are in the habit of doing, but encouraging one another—and all the more as you see the Day approaching. (Hebrews 10:25 NIV)

Responsible people connect!

3. Responsible People Care and Carry

One of the major characteristics of a responsible person is a willingness to properly care for self, others, and the things you're given or have stewardship over. Lack of care is a sign of a lack of responsibility and maturity.

When your kids start taking care of things, you know they're learning responsibility. They start taking baths and brushing their teeth without you reminding them (miracle!). It's a signal that they're growing up. Later you see them take care of an animal, or a bike, and perhaps a car. As they grow in responsibility, they stop treating things carelessly. They become aware of value and handle things with greater care.

Care is a necessary quality for those called by God to carry out the mission and work of the church. If you don't really care, you won't be a strong and useful partner with God.

Care for the church is critical to serving the church well. Paul the apostle wrote about the importance of caring for the church:

> Then, besides all this, I have the daily burden of my concern for all the churches. (2 Corinthians 11:28 NLT)
>
> I hope in the Lord Jesus to send Timothy to you soon, that I also may be cheered when I receive news about you. I have no one else like him, who will show genuine concern for your welfare. For everyone looks out for their own interests, not those of Jesus Christ. But you know that Timothy has proved himself, because as a son with his father he has served with me in the work of the gospel. (Philippians 2:19-22 NIV)

Paul highly valued Timothy because of Timothy's deep care for the church. Paul had lots of relationships, but when talking about Timothy, he said, "I have no one else like him" (Philippians 2:20 NIV). What was it about Timothy that set him apart from others? It was his genuine concern for the welfare of the church.

Paul was concerned for all of the churches every single day. He cared—so much so that he compared his caring to the pangs of childbirth (Galatians 4:19). It is not enough just to be connected; we need to develop a heart that really cares.

Care, or the lack of it, says a lot about you. Care shows how much you value and appreciate something or someone. Care reveals that you understand worth. Care demonstrates how you think and feel about something or someone.

Care is not only what you actively do; it's also what you purposely refuse to do. When you care:

- You don't ignore or neglect.
- You don't damage or destroy.
- You don't harm or hinder.
- You don't disrespect or diminish.
- You don't dishonor or disgrace.

If you care for your children, you don't ignore or neglect them. If you care for your local church, you will refuse to damage or destroy it, harm or hinder it, disrespect or diminish it, dishonor or disgrace it. You'll make choices that demonstrate your care.

Jesus emphasized the importance of caring for:

- The things we're given.
- The opportunities we're provided.
- The responsibilities we're assigned.

> Whoever can be trusted with very little can also be trusted with much, and whoever is dishonest with very little will also be dishonest with much. So if you have not been trustworthy in handling worldly wealth, who will trust you with true riches? And if you have not been trustworthy with someone else's property, who will give you property of your own? (Luke 16:10-12 NIV)

Jesus tests us on this. He wants us to learn the principle of caring for what we're given. When we do, he sees that we're maturing and acting responsibly. We demonstrate that we're ready for more responsibility.

Jesus is saying if you won't take little things seriously, then you can't be trusted with larger things. I've seen many gifted, talented people trip over this principle and miss greater opportunities in God's Kingdom. They failed to be faithful in the little things, so they missed the bigger things. When I see people serving faithfully, joyously behind the scenes, moving equipment, vacuuming floors, changing diapers, and parking cars, I know that they are destined for bigger things. Taking care of the little things is an important thing with Jesus, and for your life.

The principle works, no matter who you are or where you are. Former Disney executive Al Weiss started at age eighteen cleaning up after the horses in the daily Disney parades. He embraced each opportunity and eventually became the president of Disney World and ultimately the president of worldwide operations for all Disney parks. How? He took care of the little things. He cared enough to clean those streets, and continued taking care of the small things throughout his career until he finally retired at the very top.

There are no *little jobs* in the local church. Your ministry is as important as the pastor's. One may have an up-front responsibility, others a behind-the-scenes responsibility, but your assignment is important. Do it with care.

I love the story of the Good Samaritan (Luke 10:25-37). A man is beaten up and left on the roadside to die. A Levite sees him and passes on the other side. A priest does the same. Then, one of the hated Samaritans—the people the Israelites shunned—ministered to the man, picked him up, put him on his own donkey, and carried him over the rough roads to a place of help and healing.

Maybe the Levite mumbled, "I care—God bless you." The priest could have whispered, "I care—hope you get well." But it was the Samaritan who showed he *really* cared. He carried the man. He used his own donkey. He found an inn where the man could be cared for and paid for it with his own money. Out of his *care*, he *carried*.

Responsible people carry loads. If you *care*, you'll *carry*!

Demas, in the Bible, had been a great helper to Paul. At some point, for unknown reasons, Demas stopped caring about the work of God and stopped carrying his responsibilities with Paul. Paul described it this way:

> For Demas, because he loved this world, has deserted me and has gone to Thessalonica. Crescens has gone to Galatia, and Titus to Dalmatia. (2 Timothy 4:10 NIV)

The Greek word for "deserted" means "to leave, abandon, to leave behind; to let one down."[6] Demas dropped the load on Paul and walked away. He let Paul down by failing to carry out his commitment. Paul had to pick up what Demas dropped. Demas was irresponsible, but it was Paul and the church that suffered because of it.

It would be like four of us carrying a grand piano, then one of the four just lets go. He says, "I don't want to do this anymore. I don't care." So now three people have to absorb what four people were meant to carry. This is exactly what Demas did. Demas dropped his responsibilities. He let go of the weight he should have carried.

It's no different when we serve together. When someone irresponsibly drops the weight they're supposed to shoulder, the load still has to be carried. What was meant to be carried by four people is now being carried by three. Maybe it can still be carried, but not as effectively or as quickly as it would or should have been. The job may not get done or its accomplishment might be seriously delayed.

Each assignment is critical. There are no small jobs, regardless of how they may seem to us. God and people are depending on us. Jesus is testing to see if we can qualify to move up to bigger responsibilities. So when you get an assignment in the Kingdom, be responsible, and don't drop the weight on others.

4. Responsible People Contribute

Being a responsible part of a team, organization, or group also calls for contribution. Responsible people add value, release resources, and sow generously into what they're committed to. Jesus was very clear: "For where your treasure is, there your heart will be also" (Matthew 6:21 NIV).

The apostle Paul demonstrated this kind of responsibility in his ministry. He never looked for what he could *get*, but rather what he could *give*. You'll never find a place in the New Testament where Paul was looking for how he would benefit from ministry. In fact, he demonstrated the exact opposite attitude:

> For we speak as messengers approved by God to be entrusted with the Good News. Our purpose is to please God, not people. He alone examines the motives of our hearts. Never once did we try to win you with flattery, as you well know. And God is our witness that we were not pretending to be your friends just to get your money! As for human praise, we have never sought it from you or anyone else. As apostles of Christ we certainly had a right to make some demands of you, but instead we were like children among you.
>
> Or we were like a mother feeding and caring for her own children. We loved you so much that we shared with you not only God's Good News but our own lives, too. Don't you remember, dear brothers and sisters, how hard we worked among you? Night and day we toiled to earn a living so that we would not be a burden to any of you as we preached God's Good News to you. You yourselves are our witnesses—and so is God—that we were devout and honest and faultless toward all of you believers. And you know that we treated each of you as a father treats his own children. We pleaded with you, encouraged you, and urged you to live your lives in a way that God would consider worthy. For he called you to share in his Kingdom and glory. (1 Thessalonians 2:4-12 NLT)

I am grateful, honored, and blessed to know so many people with pure motives like Paul described. Their goal is to see how much value they can add through their service, not how much benefit they can get from it. This is how it should be.

The church, through Jesus Christ, is *the* hope of the whole world. That's why it's so important to add value to it. Our communities and the world beyond are depending on us.

Paul challenged believers to be generous contributors to the work of God with their:

- Time
- Treasure
- Talent

In the following passage, we find a great example of giving. The church in Jerusalem was facing very difficult times. Other churches decided to send an offering to help them. The churches in an area known as Macedonia, which included the church at Philippi, were also facing their own challenges. Yet, with great joy and tremendous generosity they begged Paul to be a part of this offering for their brothers and sisters in Jerusalem. This impressed Paul so much that he used them as a positive example of giving for other churches to follow. Look at what he wrote about them:

> And now, brothers and sisters, we want you to know about the grace that God has given the Macedonian churches. In the midst of a very severe trial, their overflowing joy and their extreme poverty welled up

in rich generosity. For I testify that they gave as much as they were able, and even beyond their ability. Entirely on their own, they urgently pleaded with us for the privilege of sharing in this service to the Lord's people. And they exceeded our expectations: They gave themselves first of all to the Lord, and then by the will of God also to us. So we urged Titus, just as he had earlier made a beginning, to bring also to completion this act of grace on your part. But since you excel in everything—in faith, in speech, in knowledge, in complete earnestness and in the love we have kindled in you—see that you also excel in this grace of giving.

I am not commanding you, but I want to test the sincerity of your love by comparing it with the earnestness of others. For you know the grace of our Lord Jesus Christ, that though He was rich, yet for your sake He became poor, so that you through his poverty might become rich.

And here is my judgment about what is best for you in this matter. Last year you were the first not only to give but also to have the desire to do so. Now finish the work, so that your eager willingness to do it may be matched by your completion of it, according to your means. For if the willingness is there, the gift is acceptable according to what one has, not according to what one does not have. (2 Corinthians 8:1-12 NIV)

Paul continued by reminding us of the attitude we should have in our giving, and the blessings that come when we give generously and joyously.

> Remember this: Whoever sows sparingly will also reap sparingly, and whoever sows generously will also reap generously. Each of you should give what you have decided in your heart to give, not reluctantly or under compulsion, for God loves a cheerful giver. And God is able to bless you abundantly, so that in all things at all times, having all that you need, you will abound in every good work. (2 Corinthians 9:6-8 NIV)

Contributing is part of family life. A responsible family member contributes to the family. An important question to continually consider is, "What contribution am *I* making to my spiritual family? Am I generously and joyously giving of my time, treasure, and talents to God and his church?"

For every Christian, part of the basics of giving is learning to tithe. Tithing is God's beginning point in giving. Tithing is simply returning to God the first ten percent of the resources you earn or receive.

Giving is a *big* deal to God. It's part of his nature—God is a giver. Giving is important to us because it leads to *big* spiritual growth. Each time you give, you're saying, "I trust God." Tithing starts you on the giving journey. It demonstrates and increases your trust in God.

Tithing acknowledges that all we have, including our ability to earn a living, comes from and belongs to God. Tithing is a key step of faith and obedience. Tithing prepares us for greater responsibility.

"Tithing is for the health of the believer, not the health of the church," men's minister Ed Cole often said. God is not trying to get something *from* you. He is trying to get something *in* you. *Everything you do with God will come through a step of faith.* Tithing is a practical step of faith. Tithing is never about your *money*. It's always about your *heart*.

Look at the promise God gives to those who take this step of faith:

> "Will a mere mortal rob God? Yet you rob me. But you ask, 'How are we robbing you?' In tithes and offerings. You are under a curse—your whole nation—because you are robbing me. Bring the whole tithe into the storehouse, that there may be food in my house. Test me in this," says the Lord Almighty, "and see if I will not throw open the floodgates of heaven and pour out so much blessing that there will not be room enough to store it. I will prevent pests from devouring your crops, and the vines in your fields will not drop their fruit before it is ripe," says the Lord Almighty. "Then all the nations will call you blessed, for yours will be a delightful land," says the Lord Almighty (Malachi 3:8-12 NIV).

Jesus reinforced this principle of tithing in his teaching:

> What sorrow awaits you teachers of religious law and you Pharisees. Hypocrites! For you are careful to

> tithe even the tiniest income from your herb gardens, but you ignore the more important aspects of the law—justice, mercy, and faith. You should tithe, yes, but do not neglect the more important things (Matthew 23:23 NLT).

Tithing needs to be a consistent part of the life of everyone who serves, and something you're prepared to teach and inspire others to do. As you take this step of faith and obedience and experience the blessings that come as a result, make sure you pass the lessons on to others.

One of the most beautiful contribution stories in the Bible is the story of King David's purchase of land to build an altar to God. God called David to build an altar on a piece of property owned by a man named Araunah. When King David approached Araunah about buying the land, Araunah said he'd freely give David the threshing floor, and in addition provide oxen, wood, and wheat for worship. But David said, "No, I insist on paying the full price. I will not take for the Lord what is yours, or sacrifice a burnt offering that costs me nothing" (1 Chronicles 21:24 NIV).

David basically said, "I'm not going to sacrifice to God that which cost me nothing." *In other words, a sacrifice is not a sacrifice unless you sacrificed to give it.* This is profound.

David could have accepted the land without cost, but he understood that *the depth of his worship would be affected and demonstrated by the degree of his contribution.* He refused the temptation to "take." Instead, he *gave*. He was a contributor.

Responsible people contribute. They invest time, treasure and talents into the work of their local church and the advance of the Kingdom of God.

5. Responsible People Celebrate

People who responsibly partner with God are rewarded by God. There's nothing more fulfilling than investing yourself in God's work—perhaps by ushering, or driving a shuttle bus, or leading a group, or teaching a child—only to see your little investment bring a huge return in someone's life. Serving God and people is the path to joy.

People sometimes think that responsibility is a dull, boring, and difficult thing, so they avoid it. But when you really think about it, avoiding responsibility is the surest pathway to misery. Refusing to be responsible for your health usually results in bad health. Refusing to be responsible for your money results in little or no money. *Irresponsibility costs us. Responsibility blesses us. A responsible life is a joyous life.*

Jesus gave us the parable of the prodigal son. It's about a young man who demanded his family inheritance. He wanted to rid himself of all responsibility, have a good time, and do whatever he wanted. He took the money and headed into the world of irresponsibility, only to experience a crash landing with reality. His life was miserable and his inheritance was wasted, all because he wanted a carefree, irresponsible life (see Luke 15:11-24).

At his darkest moment, the young man finally understood that life was a lot better, even as a servant, in an environment of responsibility. He headed home intending to become his father's servant, only to find that his father received his returned son with celebration.

Some Christians have little joy in their lives because they haven't embraced spiritual responsibility. It's hard to celebrate the great, wonderful things God does if you haven't invested in making it happen.

Remember the parable of the talents (Matthew 25:14-30). The person with five talents doubled what he was given. The person with two talents doubled what he was given. The person with one did nothing. The faithful servants learned that responsible living is the way to experience the highest joy in life:

> His master replied, "Well done, good and faithful servant! You have been faithful with a few things; I will put you in charge of many things. Come and share your master's happiness!" (Matthew 25:21 NIV)

Joy comes when you fulfill your responsibilities. Doing your part, and doing it well positions you to celebrate the wins, and deeply appreciate the results of your efforts.

Power Points

- Partnership with God requires accepting responsibility.
- Everybody has a part to play in the building of Jesus' church.
- A responsible person has five characteristics:

  1. Commits
  2. Connects
  3. Cares and carries
  4. Contributes
  5. Celebrates

Power Prayer

Father, thank you for offering me the privilege of partnership.

Give me the strength of character and determination to accept responsibility in my church.

Help me each day to commit, connect, care, carry, and contribute in the name of Jesus, Amen.

Chapter 4

Be Extraordinary in Your Service

One of the wonderful things God gives us in life is *opportunity*. What we do with opportunities, whether they seem great or small, is important to our development and to our future. It's been said, "Small doors often open to large rooms."

The Nature of Opportunities

Opportunities Are Often Tests

God watches what we do with what we're given. As I look back over my life, I see lots of testing moments centered around opportunities. Most of the ministry opportunities that paved the path to my current ministry role initially appeared little, mundane, and unimportant—something that I could've pushed aside and rejected. But in retrospect, I realize that these seemingly small opportunities were tests and training points in my life. God was watching my response, and my future was being determined by how I handled them.

The key is found in this one verse:

> Whatever you do, work at it with all your heart, as working for the Lord, not for human masters. (Colossians 3:23 NIV)

When I recognize that I'm working primarily for God, I automatically want to work extra hard, no matter how large or small the task. I want to give him my very best. Reminding myself of this brings out something more than ordinary. I am called, challenged, and encouraged to be extraordinary!

Note how God expects us to handle the opportunities he sends our way:

> Now in this way those who are trusted with something valuable must show they are worthy of that trust. (1 Corinthians 4:2 NCV)

> And, oh, yes, tell Archippus, "Do your best in the job you received from the Master. Do your very best." (Colossians 4:17 MSG)

Every Opportunity Has a Weight and Value

It's important that we give every opportunity the appropriate weight and value it deserves.

So often we serve in roles that no one ever knows about. But looking back, we can see how God was doing something good in our character, growing us, testing our faithfulness, and training us to be better and stronger. Opportunities many times don't happen in the spotlight. *But just because opportunities aren't visible doesn't mean they're not valuable.*

Opportunities Have a Lifetime

We've all heard it said that someone was given "the opportunity of a lifetime." But *every* opportunity is an opportunity of a lifetime because it's actually preparing us for our next one. And, every opportunity *has* a lifetime. If I'm not prepared to embrace an opportunity when it presents itself, I'll miss it. I will also miss the future possibilities that may have been birthed by it. The best time to prepare for opportunities is before they arrive.

The Life of Daniel

Perhaps no one in Scripture exemplified the proper handling of God-given opportunities any better than Daniel. As a young man,

Daniel was torn away from his homeland in Judah and taken to a foreign country, Babylon, to serve a foreign and pagan king. Daniel was entrusted with a variety of duties and roles over the course of his life and work there. He often served in hidden, non-glamorous places. Daniel could have viewed these circumstances as horrible catastrophes in his life. But in reality, they were God-given opportunities.

Daniel had a choice; he could have become bitter about being exiled to Babylon. He could have adopted a victim mentality, faded into obscurity, and lived a life of mediocrity. But Daniel didn't do this. He took the situations handed to him and accepted them. He applied himself to what was before him with diligence, faithfulness, and excellence. As a result, God raised him to a place of great prominence and usefulness in his Kingdom.

Daniel's primary jobs in Babylon were administration, management and, ultimately, significant leadership. Because Daniel excelled in his duties, he became a key influencer in government, and a great role model to many. His example has continued for millennia. We're still reading and talking about him today.

Daniel was consistently promoted, no matter who he was serving and what responsibilities he was performing. Daniel's response to small opportunities became a pathway to greater ones. He rose to the occasion in every situation, no matter how challenging or difficult. He was at the top of the top of the class; the *crème de la crème*.

Cautionary Tales

History records some huge blunders people have made with opportunities they were given. Christopher Columbus, for one, possessed incredible faith and perseverance as he set out from Portugal to find gold for his patron king and queen. Bravely conquering the hardships of the unknown and frightening open seas, Columbus sailed to the New World. Yet he died without ever knowing what he had truly discovered. Blinded by a search for gold, and failing to find the bounty he longed for, he settled for opening new routes for the slave trade. He never realized he'd found the New World. Columbus historian Justin Winsor states, "Hardly another character in the world's record has made so little of its opportunities."[7]

Inspiring Deeds

On the other hand, some people have made a mark on history with the barest of opportunities. Retired ice skater and committed Christian Scott Hamilton had an undiagnosed brain tumor through much of his childhood that caused him to stop growing. Yet he kept training. When he didn't have the finances to compete, a philanthropic couple gave him his opportunity. He was ready for that opportunity and had an illustrious career, winning Olympic gold for the US.

The point is this—*look at your own opportunities*. Do some seem more exciting and enjoyable than others? Do some seem like more work than others? Don't let work worry you. Not every opportunity that's good for you is going to be fun for you. Apply yourself diligently to everything God assigns you. You never know where any assignment will take you until you give it that extra effort.

How to Be a Go-To Person in God's Kingdom

What characteristics did Daniel possess that caused him to consistently rise to the top? The following verse tells us a lot about him:

> There was no one quite like him. He could do anything—interpret dreams, solve mysteries, explain puzzles. His name is Daniel, but he was renamed Belteshazzar by the king. Have Daniel called in. He'll tell you what is going on here. (Daniel 5:12 MSG)

> Inasmuch as an excellent spirit, knowledge, understanding, interpreting dreams, solving riddles, and explaining enigmas were found in this Daniel, whom the king named Belteshazzar, now let Daniel be called, and he will give the interpretation. (Daniel 5:12 NKJV)

> This man Daniel, whom the king named Belteshazzar, has exceptional ability and is filled with divine knowledge and understanding. He can interpret dreams, explain riddles, and solve difficult problems. Call for Daniel, and he will tell you what the writing means. (Daniel 5:12 NLT)

The Bible says that:

- Daniel had an excellent spirit.
- Daniel excelled in knowledge and understanding.
- Daniel applied his gifts by interpreting dreams, explaining hard and complex subjects, and by dissolving the doubts and fears of others.

Daniel was known to people around him as the go-to guy. He worked diligently and demonstrated excellence in everything he did. He valued excellence. He was committed to the extraordinary.

The backstory to Daniel 5:12 is fascinating. The king of Babylon was having a wild party packed with people. During the party, something strange and eerie suddenly happened—mysterious human fingers appeared and wrote on a wall. Everyone was frightened and confused, especially the king. Take a look at the story:

> King Belshazzar gave a great banquet for a thousand of his nobles and drank wine with them. While Belshazzar was drinking his wine, he gave orders to bring in the gold and silver goblets that Nebuchadnezzar his father had taken from the temple in Jerusalem, so that the king and his nobles, his wives and his concubines might drink from them. So they brought in the gold goblets that had been taken from the temple of God in Jerusalem, and the king and his nobles, his wives and his concubines drank from them. As they drank the wine, they praised the gods of gold and silver, of bronze, iron, wood

> and stone. Suddenly the fingers of a human hand appeared and wrote on the plaster of the wall, near the lampstand in the royal palace. The king watched the hand as it wrote. His face turned pale and he was so frightened that his legs became weak and his knees were knocking. The king summoned the enchanters, astrologers and diviners. Then he said to these wise men of Babylon, "Whoever reads this writing and tells me what it means will be clothed in purple and have a gold chain placed around his neck, and he will be made the third highest ruler in the kingdom." Then all the king's wise men came in, but they could not read the writing or tell the king what it meant. So King Belshazzar became even more terrified and his face grew more pale. His nobles were baffled. (Daniel 5:1-9 NIV)

The king of Babylon needed someone to interpret the frightening handwriting on the wall. It was the queen who said, "I know someone that can do this job!" Wow! Daniel was known in the inner circle of royalty because of the kind of man he was.

Daniel had a reputation. He had consistently and carefully managed the opportunities he had been given to this point. He had a good track record. This reputation provided him a new opportunity.

To be like Daniel, we must be go-to people. When people wonder, "Who can take on this responsibility?" we want to be the one they think of. Daniel was that guy.

> The queen, hearing the voices of the king and his nobles, came into the banquet hall. "O king, live forever!" she said. "Don't be alarmed! Don't look so pale! There is a man in your kingdom who has the spirit of the holy gods in him. In the time of your father he was found to have insight and intelligence and wisdom like that of the gods. King Nebuchadnezzar your father—your father the king, I say—appointed him chief of the magicians, enchanters, astrologers and diviners." (Daniel 5:10, 11 NIV)

Daniel was chosen for the job because he was an extraordinary person.

How to Make the Most of Every Opportunity

What can we learn from Daniel that will help us make the most of the opportunities God gives us? How can we become that go-to man or woman in the local church and in the Kingdom of God?

See and Seize Opportunities When They Appear

Never forget that tomorrow's open doors depend on how we handle today's opportunities.

Every person is given a unique set of opportunities. *Your current role and responsibilities are your opportunities*. It's what God has given you right now, for a specific *reason* and for a specific *season*. How you handle them will determine the trajectory of your future.

It's so easy to get ahead of ourselves. When we are "here" we want to be "there." We tend to look at the "there and then" and forget about the "here and now."

God challenges you to live in the moment—in your now. Some current opportunities may seem hard and mundane. But guess what? When you step into your future you'll discover that it looks very much like your now—hard work and a lot of mundane! Remember, every time you get to your next "there and then" it becomes your "here and now." The only time you ever really have in your life is the "here and now." And how you're handling it matters a lot.

A vision of the future always looks a lot more glamorous than it actually is. While vision is valuable, the fulfillment of vision requires embracing the moment and seizing present opportunities with excellence.

For example, every time our church has launched additional campuses or ministries, it was exciting, fulfilling, even thrilling. The vision was inspiring. But it also ended up being a lot of unseen, unrecognized, early-morning-to-late-night hard work. Do we regret pursuing the vision? Of course not. But it underscores the fact that when your dreams become realities, you find yourself pretty much doing the same thing you've always done—handling responsibilities.

Opportunities have weight to them. The opportunity you're in now is strengthening your character. It's building you for your future.

Develop an Extraordinary Spirit

Another thing we notice about Daniel is his *extraordinary spirit* (Daniel 6:3). Somewhere I read that the word "extraordinary" comes from an ancient term, which means a jutting rock. It refers to something that stands out in a clear and obvious way.

The word describes qualities that are *uncommon*, beyond what is usual. To be extraordinary is to be exceptional. It means not just going the first mile and meeting basic requirements, doing what's asked of us, but going beyond what is expected. It's being the person that doesn't just talk the talk but walks the walk. You over-deliver on what is required or expected.

What was extraordinary about Daniel? His spirit.

"Spirit" refers to what is in us that comes out of us, especially when tested. Our spirit is the substance of who we are. It is formed through life experiences, and how we handle them.

As believers, our spirit is developed through time alone with God (or the absence of it) and by the way we respond to God's dealings with us. Our spirit is formed by the moral choices we make, the attitudes we adopt, the habits we develop, and the people we surround ourselves with. It's the attitudes we demonstrate and the atmosphere we create by who we are and how we approach life.

We each have an individual spirit. The collection of all the spirits in a local church creates the spirit of that church. It's what people see and feel when exposed to the people and ministries of the church. Our spirit can be good or bad, positive or negative, but *everyone* and *every group* has a spirit about them.

Daniel had a spirit that was highly unusual in an extremely positive way. This can be seen in the way he responded to the king's request for Daniel to interpret the strange writing on the wall. Look at how Daniel handled this difficult situation:

> "Now I have heard that you are able to give interpretations and to solve difficult problems. If you can read this writing and tell me what it means, you will be clothed in purple and have a gold chain placed around your neck, and you will be made the third highest ruler in the kingdom." Then Daniel answered the king, "You may keep your gifts for

> yourself and give your rewards to someone else. Nevertheless, I will read the writing for the king and tell him what it means." (Daniel 5:16, 17 NIV)

When the king offered Daniel position and money for his wisdom, Daniel said: "No, thanks!" Daniel was not greedy, self-serving, or opportunistic. He had the right motives. Daniel had a clean and right heart. He was giving and serving with no expectation of return.

God wants you to be like Daniel. He wants you to have an extraordinary spirit. People like this are a rare find, and a great asset to the Kingdom of God.

Keep Growing in Knowledge, Understanding, and Wisdom

Daniel was extraordinary in his knowledge, understanding, and wisdom. People consistently observed these qualities in this young man. The Bible says, "Daniel was found to have a keen mind and knowledge and understanding" (Daniel 5:12 NIV).

Daniel was a knowledgeable man. He understood his job well. He was wise. He made prudent decisions.

Knowledge, understanding, and wisdom don't just show up in a person's life. They are the result of a person's spirit. They are the result of a person's determined pursuit to discover and grow. For God to continue to bring opportunities into our lives, we have to make sure that we are personally and proactively investing in the increase of knowledge, wisdom, and understanding.

Knowledge, understanding, and wisdom come when we study, listen, reflect, contemplate, and lean into people that can help us learn and grow. These things come to people who diligently apply themselves to gaining them.

Look at the value God places on gaining knowledge, understanding, and wisdom:

> Choose my instruction instead of silver, knowledge rather than choice gold. (Proverbs 8:10 NIV)
>
> The wise store up knowledge, but the mouth of a fool invites ruin. (Proverbs 10:14 NIV)
>
> Apply your heart to instruction and your ears to words of knowledge. (Proverbs 23:12 NIV)
>
> The beginning of wisdom is this: Get wisdom. Though it cost all you have, get understanding. (Proverbs 4:7 NIV)
>
> Gold there is, and rubies in abundance, but lips that speak knowledge are a rare jewel. (Proverbs 20:15 NIV)
>
> But grow in the grace and knowledge of our Lord and Savior Jesus Christ. To him be glory both now and forever! Amen. (2 Peter 3:18 NIV)

God says, "Even if it costs us everything, go after wisdom!" Knowledge and wisdom come with applied study. They come with late nights, early mornings, and a willingness to pay the price to learn and grow.

Daniel was chosen by the king for this assignment because he was a good student. He disciplined himself. He prepared himself. Because of this, greater opportunity came his way. Remember, opportunities come to the *prepared*. We must be prepared before an opportunity shows up; otherwise, we will miss it when it comes our way. Once an opportunity for additional responsibility arrives, it's too late to get ready for it.

Increase and Improve Your Skills and Abilities

A key mark of an extraordinary person is the conscious development and growth of their skills. Scripture says, "Daniel was found to have … the ability to interpret dreams, explain riddles and solve difficult problems" (Daniel 5:12 NIV). Another translation says, "This man Daniel … has exceptional ability and is filled with divine knowledge and understanding. He can interpret dreams, explain riddles, and solve difficult problems" (Daniel 5:12 NLT).

Knowledge, understanding, and wisdom don't always translate into actual abilities or proficient practical skills. Knowledge is what you know. Abilities are what you do with what you know.

Think about sports. I can study a playbook, study the *rules*, and know every detail about a sport and still be useless on the field. I can talk a big game and know exactly how to run every play and still not be capable of executing. It's one thing to have knowledge in your *head* but a completely different thing to have skills in your *hand*.

We need both.

Daniel had knowledge and understanding, and he also developed his abilities and used them effectively. He studied the things that were necessary to do his job well, but he also developed strong, practical skills. He excellently executed what he had learned.

A person with an excellent spirit is always growing their skill set, improving their proficiencies, monitoring their effectiveness and efficiencies, and developing increased capacity for usefulness. They are always self-assessing. They're asking themselves, "Am I getting better at what I am doing?" They keep on getting better at what they do, and before long, they're doing more than they ever thought they would!

Note what God says about a person who develops their skills and abilities:

> Do you see a man who excels in his work? He will stand before kings; He will not stand before unknown men. (Proverbs 22:29 NKJV)
>
> Do you see any truly competent workers? They will serve kings rather than working for ordinary people. (Proverbs 22:29 NLT)

Here are five steps to developing your abilities:

- ***Step One: Use What You Have***

Don't focus on what you don't have. God has given each of us specific resources. We develop our abilities by using what God has given to us in this moment, rather than focusing on what we don't have, could have, or should have. It's dangerous to fail to use what you have. Jesus declares, "To those who use well what they are given, even more will be given, and they will have an abundance. But from those who do nothing, even what little they have will be taken away" (Matthew 25:29 NLT).

- ***Step Two: Embrace New, Stretching Opportunities, Responsibilities, and Challenges***

Don't shy away from new, challenging, stretching opportunities. Run toward them.

David *ran* toward Goliath. He didn't wait for Goliath. What others were running away *from*, he ran *toward*. Others may have seen Goliath as an *obstacle*, but David saw him as an *opportunity*.

Sometimes we shy away from accepting more responsibility or more opportunities, but the extraordinary spirit looks for stretching opportunities.

- ***Step Three: Practice, Practice, Practice***

Do the legwork of learning. "Practice makes perfect," we've all heard. Think about it another way—practice also makes *permanent*. How you practice is how you play. What you practice and how well you practice determines what becomes part of you.

Daniel was extraordinary because he continually increased and improved his skills and abilities. He improved himself. If you are a singer, improve your singing. If you are an usher or greeter, improve your people skills. If you operate the audio, learn and grow so that you excel. Whatever opportunity God has given you, practice, practice, practice!

- ***Step Four: Pay Attention to Good Examples and Teachers***

Turn your environment into a training lab. Remember, when Joseph was in an Egyptian prison, the prison became his graduate school. You're in training right now. What is God preparing you for? Where you are right now is the training lab God is using for where you're going.

- ***Step Five: Never Give Anything Less Than Your Best. Be a Second-Mile Servant.***

When someone asks you to clean a room, don't do the minimum required. Go beyond what is required. When the leader comes back, let them see you've not only cleaned the room but the bathroom, too!

Be a Problem Solver

The Bible says that Daniel knew how to solve difficult problems. "Inasmuch as an excellent spirit, knowledge, understanding, interpreting dreams, solving riddles, and explaining enigmas were found in this Daniel ... now let Daniel be called, and he will give the interpretation" (Daniel 5:12 NKJV). "Daniel ... was found to have a keen mind and knowledge and understanding, and also the ability to interpret dreams, explain riddles and solve difficult problems" (Daniel 5:12 NIV).

Daniel was a problem solver. When it comes to problems, ordinary people fall into three basic categories:

- ***Producers***

These people need no explanation; we've all met them. They produce problems practically everywhere they go.

- ***Identifiers***

These folks are good at identifying problems—in everyone but themselves.

- ***Complainers***

These individuals may not cause problems, but they sure can identify them and grumble about them.

Problem producers, identifiers, and complainers attract people with a similar spirit. They gravitate toward one another and their impact can be devastating.

Don't be a problem producer, identifier, or complainer. Be a problem solver. Bring an excellent spirit into your environment. Give a different perspective. Hold a high standard. Step in and lift the spirit. Work to solve the problems.

The Hebrew term for "solve" means "to loosen." This is what problem solvers do. They untangle problems and bring timely, trustworthy answers and resolutions.

One of the greatest things we can become in life is a problem solver. True problem solvers are hard to find. These qualities quickly separate people from the rest of the pack and identify them for promotion.

Here are some things that will make you a better problem solver:

- ***Accept Responsibility for Solutions***

It's a mark of maturity to see a problem and immediately accept responsibility to find the solution for it.

- ***Pray***

As we pray, God gives us vision and clarity. He shows us solutions.

- ***Think***

It's enormously practical and obvious, but many people never really think. Instead, they saturate their minds with music, media, or noise, and never learn how to think through things. You can't solve problems without thinking. Learn to think, and spend time doing it.

- ***Explore***

For every problem, there are likely multiple solutions. Problem solvers explore the depth and breadth of possibilities for solving a problem or making something better.

- ***Execute***

It's a special, unique gift to confront problems, face challenges, and look at seemingly impossible issues—and not be discouraged by them. Problem solvers overcome this hurdle. They use all available means to change things for the better. They engage in positive action. They execute solutions. They roll up their sleeves and get to work helping. Problem solvers are persistent. They don't give up until the solution is in place. And they execute solutions with a pleasant, faith-filled attitude.

- ***Increase Your Value***

Be a person who grows in value to the people you serve. Be a greater help and blessing today than you were yesterday. Like Daniel, make it your goal to be a go-to person in whatever you do.

It's not an accident that God has put specific, unique opportunities before you. Remember, opportunities are often challenging and uncomfortable. They require something from us. Think about Daniel. The opportunities as a servant were not glamorous, but he was faithful in them. Because of this, he developed a good reputation. He consistently went the extra mile. Daniel's name was always at the top of the promotion list.

God wants to move you from the ordinary to the extraordinary. He wants you to develop a *Daniel spirit*—an extraordinary spirit.

Being extraordinary isn't complicated. It starts with adding *extra* to the ordinary. Anyone can do this. Start adding extra into your commitments, work, and pursuits. Before long you'll develop a reputation like Daniel.

Power Points

- The nature of opportunities:
    - ◊ Opportunities are often tests.
    - ◊ Every opportunity has a weight and value.
    - ◊ Opportunities have a lifetime.
- Be the go-to person in God's Kingdom.
- Make the most of every opportunity.
    - ◊ See and seize opportunities when they appear.
    - ◊ Develop an extraordinary spirit.
    - ◊ Keep growing in knowledge, understanding, and wisdom.
    - ◊ Increase and improve your skills and abilities.
    - ◊ Be a problem solver.

Power Prayer

Father, make me a Daniel in my generation.

Let me be one of your go-to people on this earth.

Develop in me an excellent spirit.

Help me to see and seize every opportunity,

in the name of Jesus, Amen.

Chapter 5

Align with the Team

Have you ever watched a rowing competition? It's both painful and beautiful to watch. The boats glide through the water so smoothly. The rowers move their oars in such amazing unity. Every moment is in harmony. Instinctively, you know that it's not the muscle power of one person that wins the race, it's the power of a unified team.

A key part of that team is the coxswain. The coxswain is the *caller* in the back of the boat that steers it, motivates the rowers, ensures their safety, and keeps them in sync. The race depends on the physical and mental strength of the rowers, and the abilities of the coxswain. Coxswains set the atmosphere for the team. They know when their team needs motivation or silence.

Long before these individual team members can be part of the kinds of races that attract a television audience, they've had to learn a few things. The rule for rowers is "hands on, mouths shut." As soon as they take their oars, they stop talking and start listening. In other words, they learn selflessness, trust, and humility along with commitment and perseverance. It's obvious they aren't insisting on rowing their own way. If everyone did their own thing, they'd lose for sure! They subject their own plans and ideas to the mission and plans of the entire team.

Rowers row with their backs to the finish line. They're completely dependent on the coxswain's directions. They have learned to trust, to follow directions, and to know that the coxswain is directing them to the finish line as winners. This is called *alignment*. It's another word for *unity*.

You've certainly heard the old adage, "united we stand, divided we fall." This statement highlights a principle that produces success or failure in every organization or enterprise. Division is a sure pathway to defeat. Unity is the way to win. It's how people accomplish great things.

Jesus described it this way: "If a kingdom is divided against itself, that kingdom cannot stand. If a house is divided against itself, that house cannot stand" (Mark 3:24, 25 NIV).

For anything to work well and fulfill its highest potential, there must be alignment of the important and necessary parts. One part out of place can bring an entire operation to an end.

For advancement, success, productivity, and peace, alignment is not an option, it's a necessity. In business, music, or any other realm of life that requires joint effort for success, alignment is a high priority. Success is always linked to unity.

The prophet Amos posed this question long ago, "Can two walk together, except they be agreed?" (Amos 3:3 KJV). The answer is obvious. God's very own people had walked away from him. Instead of living for God, they were living for themselves. So Amos was reminding them of the principle of alignment. You can't walk with God if you're not in agreement with God. It's true in our personal relationships also. You can't walk well or work well with people you're fighting with.

If I'm pulling one way and my wife is pulling the opposite way, then obviously we'll go nowhere. Forward progress is made when we stop fighting against each other and start cooperating. It's the only way to move ahead.

What Is Alignment?

Alignment refers to agreement, unity, cooperation, proper positioning, adjustment, and submission to the right order. The opposite of alignment is disorder, division, separation, and disjointedness.

God is pro-alignment. By his very nature, he shows us the high priority and importance of it.

The God of the Bible is the Triune God. He is one, but three; three, but one. There is no "di-vision" in the Trinity. There is perfect unity—absolute alignment.

Let's look at four examples of alignment in the persons of the Trinity.

1. Jesus Spoke of His Complete Alignment with His Heavenly Father

> I and the Father are one. (John 10:30 NIV)

> Jesus replied, "Have I been with you all this time, Philip, and yet you still don't know who I am? Anyone who has seen me has seen the Father! So why are you asking me to show him to you?" (John 14:9 NLT)

Think about Jesus while he was on the earth—fully God, fully man. People said, "Show us the Father!" Jesus said in essence, "If you've seen me, what you see in me is exactly what you would see in the Father. There's no difference in how we operate, how we behave, and how we speak."

2. While on Earth, Jesus Ministered in the Power of the Holy Spirit

> You know what has happened throughout the province of Judea ... how God anointed Jesus of Nazareth with the Holy Spirit and power, and how he went around doing good and healing all who were under the power of the devil, because God was with him.
> (Acts 10:37, 38 NIV)

> Jesus ministered in the power of the Holy Spirit, doing only what God the Father directed. Jesus said in effect, "I don't speak on my own authority. The Father who sent me has commanded me what to say and how to say it." (John 12:49 NLT)

3. At Jesus' Baptism, We See the Perfect Alignment of the Father, the Son, and the Holy Spirit

> As soon as Jesus was baptized, He went up out of the water. At that moment heaven was opened, and he saw the Spirit of God descending like a dove and alighting on him. And a voice from heaven said, "This is my Son, whom I love; with him I am well pleased." (Matthew 3:16, 17 NIV)

All three persons of the Trinity showed alignment at Jesus' baptism—the Son, the Father and the Holy Spirit. The Trinity is the highest and greatest expression of unity. It is the premier model of alignment.

4. God's Desire for Unity and Alignment Is Seen in Creation

When God created humanity and ordained the institution of marriage, the emphasis was (and still is) on unity:

> So the Lord God caused the man to fall into a deep sleep; and while he was sleeping, he took one of the man's ribs and then closed up the place with flesh.

> Then the Lord God made a woman from the rib He had taken out of the man, and He brought her to the man. The man said, "This is now bone of my bones and flesh of my flesh; she shall be called 'woman,' for she was taken out of man." That is why a man leaves his father and mother and is united to his wife, and they become one flesh. Adam and his wife were both naked, and they felt no shame. (Genesis 2:21-25 NIV)

Note the call to *oneness*. After God established the universe, he created male and female to establish the basic family unit, which is marriage. Their unity was to mirror the unity of the Trinity. That's why there's such a diabolical attack against marriage and the family. It's the devil's attempt to discredit and destroy the primary building block of society, and to destroy God's plan of a husband and wife living in unity with God and each other.

Marriage is about two becoming one. Does that mean that a husband and wife lose their individual personalities and blend into some amoebic relational blob? Emphatically, "No." The Father, the Son, and the Holy Spirit all have distinct personalities, yet enjoy perfect alignment and unity. In the same way, a husband and wife come together with unique personalities, and with God's help, become an aligned team. This is God's plan for his church also.

What Happens When Relationships Lose Alignment?

In the book of Genesis, we see what happens when relationships lose alignment.

Adam and Eve after They Sinned

As soon as sin entered Adam and Eve's lives and marriage, things began to unravel. When they knew they had done wrong, they were guilty and afraid so they hid from God. They also turned on each other. Blame and shame showed up for the first time. Why did all this happen? Because they violated unity with God and with one another. The end result of this relationship break was ongoing fear, guilt, anger, strife, sickness, and death for the entire human race.

Cain and Abel

When alignment in the family fell apart, jealousy and hatred showed up in the siblings. Eventually, Cain murdered his brother Abel.

Abraham and Lot

Working our way forward in history, we find division in the relationship between Lot and his uncle, Abraham. Instead of honoring the man who had given him an incredible life opportunity, selfishness, and greed controlled Lot. Relational tension led to a very bad decision by Lot and put him in a place called Sodom and Gomorrah. The fate of that place was destruction.

The Tower of Babel

There is no Bible story that more clearly reveals the power of unity and alignment, for evil or good, than that of the Tower of Babel. Note God's commentary on the power of unity to help or harm:

> Now the whole world had one language and a common speech. As people moved eastward, they found a plain in Shinar and settled there. They said to each other, "Come, let's make bricks and bake them thoroughly." They used brick instead of stone, and tar for mortar. Then they said, "Come, let us build ourselves a city, with a tower that reaches to the heavens, so that we may make a name for ourselves; otherwise we will be scattered over the face of the whole earth." But the Lord came down to see the city and the tower the people were building. The Lord said, "*If as one people speaking the same language they have begun to do this, then nothing they plan to do will be impossible for them.*" (Genesis 11:1-6 NIV, emphasis added)

Right here, in the midst of this story, God gave us the principle of unity. He said, in essence, "When people are one in their thinking and language, there is the release of incredible possibility." Any time you find unity, you find increased levels of capability. God even said, "nothing will be impossible to them."

Although the builders of Babel had wrong-headed, self-centered reasons for building the tower, the alignment principle is still the same. God said that when people "gather together with one mind, one heart, and one voice, nothing will be impossible for them."

God acted quickly and decisively:

> "Come, let us go down and confuse their language so they will not understand each other." So the Lord scattered them from there over all the earth, and they stopped building the city. That is why it was called Babel—because there the Lord confused the language of the whole world. From there the Lord scattered them over the face of the whole earth. (Genesis 11:7-9 NIV)

To stop the people from doing something detrimental to humanity and contrary to his will, God broke their alignment. Their unity was creating evil possibilities. But the opposite is also true. When motives are right, good, and *consistent* with God's will, unity creates positive possibilities and great blessings. There's great power in alignment.

The Spiritual and Practical Benefits of Unity

The dedication of Solomon's Temple was a huge nationwide affair with musicians and trumpeters joining in unison in praise to God. That day, the temple of the Lord was filled with a cloud of God's glory. His presence was so strong that the priests could not even perform their regular service. Unity in worship welcomed a massive outpouring of God's presence.

> The trumpeters and musicians joined in unison to give praise and thanks to the Lord. Accompanied by trumpets, cymbals, and other instruments, the singers raised their voices in praise to the Lord and sang: "He is good; his love endures forever." Then the temple of the Lord was filled with the cloud, and the priests could not perform their service because of the cloud, for the glory of the Lord filled the temple of God" (2 Chronicles 5:13, 14 NIV).

Whenever people come together under the banner of Jesus Christ in unity, they always attract the anointing of God. When we submit ourselves to him and connect ourselves one with another with a unified spirit, when we lift our voice in praise to God in one accord, we attract the glory of God.

If you want to see a blessed church, find a unified church. That's why it's imperative for those who have places of responsibility in church to deeply value unity and to pursue it aggressively and appropriately.

Look at what the Psalmist said about the connection between unity and anointing:

> How good and pleasant it is when God's people live together in unity! It is like precious oil poured on the head, running down on the beard, running down on Aaron's beard, down on the collar of his robe. It is as if the dew of Hermon were falling on Mount Zion. For there the Lord bestows his blessing, even life forevermore. (Psalm 133 NIV)

Where does the Lord bestow his blessing? In the place of unity. The early church understood this principle. On the day of Pentecost, 120 believers met in an upper room in Jerusalem. They were aligned in prayer, believing and waiting for the promise Jesus gave them of the coming outpouring of the Holy Spirit.

Their unified prayer and faith were rewarded:

> When the day of Pentecost came, they were all together in one place. Suddenly a sound like the blowing of a violent wind came from heaven and filled the whole house where they were sitting. They saw what seemed to be tongues of fire that separated and came to rest on each of them. All of them were filled with the Holy Spirit and began to speak in other tongues as the Spirit enabled them. (Acts 2:1-4 NIV)

The ongoing blessings and benefits of unity were seen in the newborn church:

> They devoted themselves to the apostles' teaching and to fellowship, to the breaking of bread and to prayer. Everyone was filled with awe at the many wonders and signs performed by the apostles. All the believers were together and had everything in common. They sold property and possessions to give to anyone who had need. Every day they continued to meet together in the temple courts. They broke bread in their homes and ate together with glad and sincere hearts, praising God and enjoying the favor of all the

> people. And the Lord added to their number daily those who were being saved. (Acts 2:42-47 NIV)

Unity always brings benefits and blessings.

Division Is Dangerous

> These six things the Lord hates, yes, seven are an abomination to Him: a proud look, a lying tongue, hands that shed innocent blood, a heart that devises wicked plans, feet that are swift in running to evil, a false witness who speaks lies, and one who sows discord among brethren. (Proverbs 6:16-19 NKJV)

Here's a list of seven things God hates. This makes them extremely serious sins. Notice what's mentioned last: *sowing discord, creating division, breaking unity.* This shows how important unity is to God.

In the New Testament, we see a strong and consistent emphasis on pursuing and protecting unity. We're called to *protect* our spiritual and relational alignment. We are to do everything we can to create, maintain, and protect unity in the church.

Take a look at just a few passages that emphasize this responsibility:

> I appeal to you, brothers and sisters, in the name of our Lord Jesus Christ, that all of you agree with one another in what you say and that there be no divisions among you, but that you be perfectly united in mind and thought. (1 Corinthians 1:10 NIV)

I urge you, brothers and sisters, to watch out for those who cause divisions and put obstacles in your way that are contrary to the teaching you have learned. Keep away from them. (Romans 16:17 NIV)

As a prisoner for the Lord, then, I urge you to live a life worthy of the calling you have received. Be completely humble and gentle; be patient, bearing with one another in love. Make every effort to keep the unity of the Spirit through the bond of peace. There is one body and one Spirit, just as you were called to one hope when you were called; one Lord, one faith, one baptism; one God and Father of all, who is over all and through all and in all. (Ephesians 4:1-6 NIV)

Therefore if you have any encouragement from being united with Christ, if any comfort from his love, if any common sharing in the Spirit, if any tenderness and compassion, then make my joy complete by being like-minded, having the same love, being one in spirit and of one mind. Do nothing out of selfish ambition or vain conceit. Rather, in humility value others above yourselves, not looking to your own interests but each of you to the interests of the others. In your relationships with one another, have the same mindset as Christ Jesus. (Philippians 2:1-5 NIV)

Therefore, as God's chosen people, holy and dearly loved, clothe yourselves with compassion, kindness,

> humility, gentleness and patience. Bear with each other and forgive one another if any of you has a grievance against someone. Forgive as the Lord forgave you. And over all these virtues put on love, which binds them all together in perfect unity. Let the peace of Christ rule in your hearts, since as members of one body you were called to peace. And be thankful. (Colossians 3:12-15 NIV)

> I plead with Euodia and I plead with Syntyche to be of the same mind in the Lord. Yes, and I ask you, my true companion, help these women since they have contended at my side in the cause of the gospel, along with Clement and the rest of my co-workers, whose names are in the book of life. (Philippians 4:2, 3 NIV)

The last verse of the passage above references two women in the Philippian church who were friends and colleagues of Paul. But something came between them that they hadn't resolved. Paul wrote these words from prison. As he sat, chained to Roman guards, his heart was burdened about two ladies in a church many miles away who were feuding. He was so concerned about them, and the potential damage their spat might bring to the church, that he took time in this short letter to address them by name. He charged them, and the spiritual leadership over them, to get busy dealing with this disunity. Division is a big deal to God—and it should be to us also.

This is why he wrote these straightforward instructions:

> Warn a divisive person once, and then warn them a second time. After that, have nothing to do with them. (Titus 3:10 NIV)

Paul says to his protégé Titus, who had become a pastor, "Don't ignore division." Paul said, "When division shows up, address it."

Divisive people should be warned. What does a warning do? It tells you to pay attention, to change your behavior. A warning is not a suggestion. A warning means trouble is coming. It means something is dangerous. Paul makes it clear that an unheeded warning to a person sowing division is grounds for removing them from the fellowship. Why? Because division is a virus that, left unaddressed, spreads and kills.

Jesus Prayed for Unity in the Church

Alignment is expected and required for the church to be all it's supposed to be. Jesus made this very clear in his final recorded prayers:

> I will remain in the world no longer, but they are still in the world, and I am coming to you. Holy Father, protect them by the power of your name, the name you gave me, so that they may be one as we are one. (John 17:11 NIV)

> My prayer is not for them alone. I pray also for those who will believe in me through their message, that all of them may be one, Father, just as you are in me and I am in you. May they also be in us so that the world may believe that you have sent me. I have given them the glory that you gave me, that they may be one as we are one—I in them and you in me—so that they

> may be brought to complete unity. Then the world will know that you sent me and have loved them even as you have loved me. (John 17:20-23 NIV)

These prayers are for us. This is Jesus' desire not just for his followers 2,000 years ago, but for you and me, his followers today—unity.

Why Is Alignment So Important?

There are at least twelve reasons why alignment is important.

1. God commands alignment.

Anything that God commands, we should obey. It's the number-one reason for pursuing unity.

2. Alignment reduces friction.

Friction creates heat. It happens when things rub together. If you don't keep parts of machines properly lubricated, there will be friction. When heat builds up from friction, it causes damage. In church, a lack of unity and harmony creates friction, and damaging "heat." Alignment reduces that friction. It doesn't mean you'll never have it. It just means it's reduced.

3. Alignment lessens wear and tear.

When you're in alignment, there is a lot less wear and tear on your life. When one of the wheels on your car is out of alignment, the tires wear out a lot faster. To maintain your tires, you keep them aligned. Our staying power will be much greater in the work of the Kingdom when we stay aligned with one another.

4. Alignment adds exponential strength.

When we're aligned with people, we become stronger. In Deuteronomy, we read that one can put a thousand to flight, but two can put ten thousand to flight (Deuteronomy 32:30). Where there's unity, exponential strength is generated.

5. Alignment makes work more fun, fruitful, and fulfilling.

People singing off-key creates dissonance. Dissonance is difficult to deal with. It's unpleasant. In relationships, lack of harmony creates an unpleasant atmosphere. But harmony is pleasing. It's refreshing. It's easy to listen to voices making one sound. Unity in the church creates a pleasant, enjoyable atmosphere. It makes serving more fun, and it produces more fruit.

6. Alignment increases creativity and problem-solving capacity.

It's called synergy. When people come together around a shared goal or mission, to work on a project or to solve a problem, the product of the whole is greater than the sum of the parts.

7. Alignment gives strategic focus.

What creates a laser beam? The strict alignment of light creates a strategic focus that gives tremendous power.

8. Alignment promotes longevity.

Just look at marriage. Which kind of marriage lasts the longest, a marriage full of strife or one where they've worked out their differences along the way? Longevity in any situation is increased by unity.

9. Alignment makes our prayer life more effective.

It's hard to pray for someone when you're mad at them or bitter toward them. One of the ways the devil hinders our prayer life is through relationship tensions, resentments, and pain. When you're upset at someone, you'll be ineffective in your prayers.

10. Alignment provides us the opportunity to be part of something bigger than ourselves.

Unity is not about me. Unity is about being part of something bigger than myself. Think of the limitations of a life lived alone, or in competition and division with others, compared to a life lived in harmony with others.

11. Alignment causes us to grow in ways we can't grow alone.

To grow you have to learn to work with other people. Think again about marriage. I often tell couples that it's the first twenty-five years of marriage that are the hardest. After that, it's a breeze! Marriage generally begins with two immature people wanting their own way. But over time, if you're willing, you learn to give and to adjust. What used to be a big deal isn't anymore. The goal of unity makes you grow. It causes you to deal with things in yourself that you otherwise would never address.

12. Alignment models the nature of God and the culture of his Kingdom.

Unity is the way we show a part of heaven to the world. There's no division in heaven. That's what we want people to experience when they come into our church. We want them to experience a little bit of heaven.

Alignment Doesn't Just Happen

Alignment doesn't "just happen." We must commit ourselves to and continuously work on it. Look at what Paul said:

> As a prisoner for the Lord, then, I urge you to live a life worthy of the calling you have received. Be completely humble and gentle; be patient, bearing with one another in love. Make every effort to keep the unity of the Spirit through the bond of peace. There is one body and one Spirit, just as you were called to one hope when you were called; one Lord, one faith, one baptism; one God and Father of all, who is over all and through all and in all. (Ephesians 4:1-6 NIV)

Don't miss an important word in this passage—*effort*. Without effort, there will be no sustained unity. The natural tendency is for things to go from order to disorder, from peace to strife. It's true in relationships, too. You have to work at unity to get it and keep it.

Twelve Commitments That Foster Alignment

Here are the twelve active commitments we *must* make to each other to achieve and preserve unity in any local church.

1. We commit to the same essential beliefs.

Your church has a statement of faith. Getting on the same page with that is where it starts. John Wesley taught:

- In the essentials (of the faith), unity.
- In nonessentials, liberty.
- In all things, charity.

We don't waiver on the essentials. The essentials hold us together as Christian believers. There are doctrinal truths that are not up for debate or subject to man's ideas and opinions. There are beliefs and commitments that make a Christian a Christian. Connect with people who hold to the essentials of the faith. But some things don't matter. These are the non-essentials. There will always be differences of opinion about things that don't really matter. Don't let these things divide you from others. And in everything, show the love of God. Even in your disagreements, be loving.

2. We commit to the same core values.

We value the same things. At our church, we value things like servant-heartedness, friendliness, and generosity. We have a list of about a dozen core values. These are things that matter to us as a church family. We are unified around our family values.

3. We commit to the same corporate mission.

Our mission is the Great Commission of Jesus. This mission may be expressed in different ways in different churches, but our job is clear. We're called by Jesus to share his message with the world.

4. We commit to devote efforts and resources to the group's health and the fulfillment of its mission.

We work hard to make sure the group is strong and the mission is being fulfilled.

5. We commit to develop and demonstrate Christlike attitudes.

You can't have hellish attitudes and expect heavenly fruit. Instead, commit to growing in Christlikeness.

6. We commit to speak the same corporate language.

Every culture has a language. God's Kingdom has a language. It's a language of faith, praise, love, servanthood, and blessing. Unity is increased when we all speak the same Kingdom language.

7. We commit to quick reconciliation in our relationships.

When relationship tensions arise, we don't wait ten years to fix it. We should commit to go to each other quickly and resolve it. Reconciliation is not proving that we're right and somebody else is wrong. Reconciliation starts with humbling ourselves. One of the best things anyone can do in relationships is to give up the right to be right, and to seek forgiveness and restoration.

8. We commit to develop an "offense-less" spirit.

We strive to be "Teflon" Christians. Even when people sling mud our way, we don't let it stick to us. *It's more than just "working through stuff," we strive to get to the place where we don't even have stuff.* We're quick to forgive and move on. We live in an attitude of forgiveness because we know that no one is perfect.

9. We commit to proactively protect corporate and relational unity.

Protect means it's a proactive thing that we do. We endeavor to keep problems from becoming problems in the first place.

10. We commit to proactively promote peace.

When we see something that could stop our alignment, we don't wait for things to get worse, we promote peace in that situation.

11. We value the goal we've been given over the role we play.

We value towels over titles. We don't need titles to feel important. Jesus stooped to wipe the disciples' feet with a towel (John 13:3-17). Don't seek titles, carry towels. Don't worry about your role, contribute to the goal!

12. We commit to respond appropriately and honorably to the leadership placed over us.

When soldiers are in a battle, they don't have time for an ongoing dialogue with the general. If the general says, "I need you deployed over here," the good soldier says, "Yes sir!" In the same way, we give proper responsiveness to the spiritual leadership that God has put over us. Leaders in the church are there to build, set order and direction, and supply vision. We're blessed when we cooperate with the leaders God places over us.

The Devil Attacks Alignment

It's important to remember that the devil is a divider. In subtle, and not-so-subtle ways, Satan tries to create strife, dissension, disorder, resistance, rebellion, suspicion, and misunderstandings among believers throughout Jesus' church. This is the devil's agenda. He never stops working. He's always trying to get us mad at each other:

- Where can I sow a little dissension?
- Where can I create some disorder?

- Where can I cause some resistance?
- Where can I make someone suspicious of somebody and blind them to the facts?
- Where can I cause some misunderstandings?

The adversary works his way in among us individually and corporately. Don't be ignorant of his agenda, his devices, and his ploy to make you a part of his "divide and conquer" program.

Fifteen Ways to Preserve Unity and Defeat the Devil

These fifteen safety valves will protect you against the devil's trap of division:

1. Keep your eyes on Jesus, on the big picture, and on becoming a big person.

Reject smallness, pettiness, and pride in your life. When you keep your eyes on Jesus, he helps you see the big picture. Sometimes you won't be able to understand exactly what's happening because where people are involved, you can't be provided every detail. But if you keep your eyes on Jesus and embrace the big picture, you'll become a big person, and you'll preserve unity.

2. Give up your "right" to resent, resist, and rebel.

Sometimes we think we have the right to resent somebody. Surrender that right in prayer. Resistance and rebellion are signs of a stubborn spirit. Stubbornness destroys teamwork.

3. Forgive freely, fully, and readily.

Let's do for people what Jesus did for us.

4. Stop gossiping and stop gossip.

Guard your mouth and your ears! This is your responsibility. Don't say what you shouldn't say or have no authority to say. Don't repeat what is unfounded, untrue, or detrimental to someone. This is the devil's work.

Over forty years ago, I realized I didn't have to listen to everything people said to me; and certainly not to their gossip. It was a point of maturity for me. If someone began sharing something with me that was inappropriate, I'd either change the subject or excuse myself from the conversation. Do you know what I discovered? People stop coming to you when you're not interested in gossip. Remember, you're in charge of your mouth and ears. You're not obligated to listen to everything everybody says. And, you don't have to answer every question. The correct response to, "Did you hear about so-and-so?" is to say, "Excuse me," and perhaps walk away.

5. Don't be a fault-finder.

Pay attention to "the plank in your own eye." We all have the tendency to create lists of what everybody else needs to change. Don't concern yourself with other people's faults. Pay attention to the things that you have control over inside yourself. As Jesus declared: "Why do you look at the speck of sawdust in your brother's eye and pay no attention to the plank in your own eye?" (Luke 6:41 NIV).

6. Don't be a Pharisee.

Who caused the most trouble for Jesus? Not the sinners. It was the religious people who always acted like they were better than everyone else. Jesus recounted the story of the Pharisee and the tax collector praying in the temple in Luke 18:9-14. The publican said, "Lord forgive me, have mercy on me." The Pharisee said, "Thank you that I'm not like the tax collector over there. I do all these wonderful things." The difference between them was their attitude of heart. Jesus was tough with Pharisees, and tender with sinners. Let's have churches that repel Pharisees and attract people who want Jesus.

7. Be a problem solver, not a problem reporter.

Some folks are like news reporters for problems. Become part of the solution and not part of the problem.

8. Be a peacemaker, not a troublemaker.

One of the greatest things to have in a church are peacemakers who diffuse situations, look for common ground, and pour oil on troubled waters.

9. Be a cooperator, not a contender.

Reject smallness, pettiness, and pride in your life. Don't contend with people; cooperatewith them.

10. Be a responder, not a reactor.

If you or someone else slips up, conquer the situation with a quick and gracious response, not a reaction.

11. Be a pray-er.

When someone or something is bothering you, generally the first step is to take no step at all. Don't *do* anything—just pray. A lot of things can be fixed just by prayer. Take the time to pray. Often you'll realize in the midst of your prayer that the issue is you, not someone else.

12. Be a team player.

There's no perfect church and no perfect pastor. Learn to work things through for the good of the whole team. Do *more* than your fair share. Be extraordinary.

13. Be a burden-bearer, not a burden-creator.

Pick up loads, don't create loads for others. Help bear burdens.

14. Refuse to hinder or hurt Jesus' church—honor and help it instead.

When people hurt or hinder a church, they hurt the heart of Christ. The church is the bride of Christ. Jesus loved the church so much that He gave himself for it. Sometimes I hear people railing about their church and I think, "Don't you understand that you're actually attacking the very thing that Jesus gave his life for?" Be the person who is never going to hinder or hurt the work of the church, but who is going to help it.

15. Be grateful to be a part of God's purpose in the earth—the building of his church!

When everything is said and done, no matter how imperfect, people *are* the church. It's our privilege to be a part of what God is doing in the world.

Unity, alignment, harmony, and cooperation with God's program is God's plan for you. It's how you live and give his dream, and play your important role on God's dream team.

Be aligned!

Power Points

- What alignment truly is.
- Bad things happen when relationships lose alignment.
- There are spiritual and practical benefits of unity.
- Division is dangerous.
- Jesus prayed for unity in the church.
- Alignment is important for many reasons.
- Alignment doesn't just happen.
- There are commitments that foster alignment.
- The devil attacks alignment.
- Fifteen ways to preserve unity and defeat the devil.

Power Prayer

Lord, we ask in the name of Jesus that you would help us to let these things find their way deep into our hearts.

We know that your peace, Lord, is a part of your Kingdom work. Let your Kingdom come, let your will be done in our lives.

We want to be a part of your program of advancing your church.

We never want to hurt or hinder it in any way. Where we have violated the principle of unity in our hearts and lives, we thank you for forgiving us.

We ask that you help us to be a strong, unified church. We pray that each one of us would be a strong member of the body of Christ.

Help us to build peace in our relationships—in our families, in our marriages, and in our homes. Let the peace of God reign in each of these areas.

We thank you for it, in the name of Jesus, Amen.

Chapter 6

Multiply Yourself

For decades, astronomers struggled to solve basic questions about the universe. With Isaac Newton's discovery of gravity came the understanding that gravity always attracts. If gravity always attracts, it was reasoned, the entire universe should be drawing closer and closer together. However, by all available measurements, the universe didn't seem to be collapsing at all. Scientists were mystified.

Then, in 1929, a Caltech scientist was making measurements in the Carnegie Observatories in Pasadena. Edwin Hubble traced the "redshifts" of a number of galaxies and measured their relative distances against the apparent brightness of particular stars. When Hubble plotted the distance, he found the "redshift" increased as a function of distance. He saw the answer. The universe wasn't even close to collapsing. The universe was expanding![8]

What does this discovery indicate about our God, Creator of the Universe? It shows us that whether it's a farmer's field, the neighborhood cats, or the universe itself, multiplication is the law of God. God is a multiplier. He majors in multiplication. He created things to grow, expand, and multiply. That's *who* he is.

What do the following words have in common?

- Progress
- Maturity
- Increase
- Productivity
- Positive results
- Development

All of these terms have one thing in common—growth! Progress leads to growth. Maturity is about growth. Increase is about growth. Productivity is about growth. Positive results are about growth. Development is about growth. When the right things are done at the right time, in the right way, growth happens. Healthy things grow.

God is a "pro-growth" God. He designed all of his creation with growth potential. Growth is very important to God.

Here are five things I have learned about multiplication from the Bible. I hope they excite you as much as they do me.

Multiplication Fact 1
The Value of Growth Is Seen in God's Very First Commandment

God spoke about increase in his very first commandment: "Then God blessed them and said, 'Be fruitful and multiply. Fill the earth and govern it. Reign over the fish in the sea, the birds in the sky, and all the animals that scurry along the ground'" (Genesis 1:28 NLT).

When God created us, he gave us the ability to reproduce. Along with this capacity, he gave his instructions to multiply—a commandment to grow, to increase, to be productive!

If someone asked you, "What's the first commandment in the Bible?" you might think about the Ten Commandments. But actually, the very first commandment in the Bible happened in the Garden of Eden. God looked at Adam and Eve and said, "Be fruitful and multiply."

There's an important Bible study principle called the "Law of First Mention." It teaches us to give special attention to the first time a major topic on doctrine is mentioned in Scripture. That first mention gives us insight into all the other mentions of that law, principle, or doctrine throughout the remainder of God's Word.

The fact that God's first command was for people to "be fruitful and multiply" reveals how important multiplication is to God. God wasn't simply addressing the growth of the human population. He was teaching us a truth. He was giving us a principle—God designed us to be productive. He made us to be *multipliers*. He wants us to grow and increase. He wants the things he's given us responsibility for to grow and increase.

Many people live stagnated, unproductive lives with very little growth. They never mature into significant producers, meaningful enlargers, multipliers, or increasers. They primarily live as consumers. Their impact and influence often grow smaller, not larger, over time.

One of the main goals of the devil is to rob and diminish the possibilities and productivity of people. He loves to steal potential and shut down fruitfulness. He delights in making people tolerate status quo living. He loves to shut down increase. It's part of his counterattack against God's plan for your life. The devil knows that God designed you for enlargement, so his objective is to make your life smaller. To limit your potential.

Jesus described it this way:

> The thief's purpose is to steal, kill and destroy. My purpose is to give life in all its fullness. (John 10:10 TLB)

Multiplication Fact 2
Jesus Taught Multiplication

We find the expectation and promise of life increase in many of Jesus' teachings:

> I am the true vine, and my Father is the gardener. He cuts off every branch in me that bears no fruit, while every branch that does bear fruit he prunes so that it will be even more fruitful. You are already clean because of the word I have spoken to you. Remain in me, as I also remain in you. No branch can bear fruit by itself; it must remain in the vine. Neither can you bear fruit unless you remain in me. I am the vine; you are the branches. If you remain in me and I in you, you will bear much fruit; apart from me you can do nothing. If you do not remain in me, you are like a branch that is thrown away and withers; such branches are picked up, thrown into the fire and burned. If you remain in me and my words remain in you, ask whatever you wish, and it will be done for you. This is to my Father's glory, that you bear much fruit, showing yourselves to be my disciples. (John 15:1-8 NIV)

This passage is all about productivity. Note the progression of fruitfulness Jesus desires from his followers:

First, he said that we are to bear … *fruit*.

Then he said, as we are pruned, we'll bear … *more fruit*.

And then it is to the Father's glory that we bear … *much fruit*.

See the progression? Fruit. More fruit. Much fruit.

When you think about yourself and your role in the Kingdom of God, remember that God's plan is for you to bear fruit, *more* fruit, and finally, *much* fruit. Ever-increasing fruitfulness! That's his desire for every one of us.

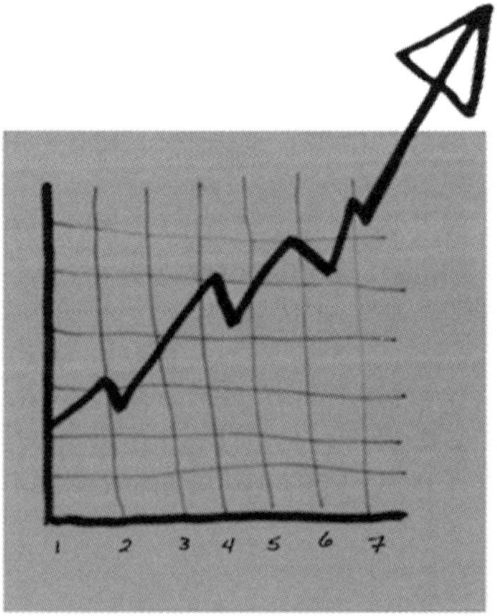

Multiplication Fact 3
Multiplication Is a Measure of Faithfulness

Jesus taught us that fruitfulness is actually a *measure* of faithfulness. He gave us a story to show us how honored God is when we're productive in the assignments, opportunities, and resources he provides us. He equates them with faithfulness. We've referenced the story before, but take time to read it.

> Again, it will be like a man going on a journey, who called his servants and entrusted his wealth to them. To one he gave five bags of gold, to another two bags, and to another one bag, each according to his ability. Then he went on his journey. The man who had received five bags of gold went at once and put his money to work and gained five bags more. So also, the one with two bags of gold gained two more. But the man who had received one bag went off, dug a hole in the ground and hid his master's money. After a long time the master of those servants returned and settled accounts with them. The man who had received five bags of gold brought the other five. "Master," he said, "you entrusted me with five bags of gold. See, I have gained five more." His master replied, "Well done, good and faithful servant! You have been faithful with a few things; I will put you in charge of many things. Come and share your master's happiness!" The man with two bags of gold also came. "Master," he said, "you entrusted me with

> two bags of gold; see, I have gained two more." His master replied, "Well done, good and faithful servant! You have been faithful with a few things; I will put you in charge of many things. Come and share your master's happiness!" Then the man who had received one bag of gold came. "Master," he said, "I knew that you are a hard man, harvesting where you have not sown and gathering where you have not scattered seed. So I was afraid and went out and hid your gold in the ground. See, here is what belongs to you." His master replied, "You wicked, lazy servant! So you knew that I harvest where I have not sown and gather where I have not scattered seed? Well then, you should have put my money on deposit with the bankers, so that when I returned I would have received it back with interest. So take the bag of gold from him and give it to the one who has ten bags. For whoever has will be given more, and they will have an abundance. Whoever does not have, even what they have will be taken from them. And throw that worthless servant outside, into the darkness, where there will be weeping and gnashing of teeth." (Matthew 25:14-30 NIV)

This passage totally changed my perspective of faithfulness. I'd always equated faithfulness with showing up. I'd learned that faithful people can be counted on because they show up for work, show up for a church service, or show up for some ministry activity. But these verses enlarged my understanding of faithfulness. Jesus didn't say, "Well done, good and faithful servant. You showed up!" No. Out of the three stewards, only two received a commendation from their master, and it wasn't for showing up, it was for growing what had been given to them. The one servant who was rebuked by the master showed up but failed to grow what had been assigned to him. The multipliers were rewarded for growth, increase, and productivity. The last servant in the story was described as a "wicked, lazy servant." The first two heard, "Well done!" The last one had to face the shame of his failure to grow.

What do you want to hear when you stand before Jesus one day? "Well done!" or "Wicked, lazy servant!" We want to hear "Well done!" But we won't hear "Well done!" unless we have done well. Well done means growth, increase, and productivity—multiplication!

From this story, we learn at least five important lessons:

First, Everybody Is Given Something to Work with in Life

You have been given gifts, opportunities, responsibilities, and resources by God. We don't all receive the *same* things, but we all receive *some* things! Everybody has something.

Second, Being an Increaser Starts with Understanding What You've Been Given by God

What gifts has God blessed you with? What opportunities has he given you? What responsibilities has he put in your hands? What resources has he provided you? Until you see and appreciate what you have, you'll never understand what you can and need to do with these things.

We spend too much time comparing what we have or don't have with what others have. We waste time fretting over our "lacks." This is counterproductive and depressing. It's one way Satan discourages and sidetracks us.

Stop for a moment and look at all the blessings God has placed in your hands. The guy with the five bags understood what he had received, "I have five bags in my hands." The guy with two knew what he'd been given, "I have two bags in my hands."

Take some time and think about what God has put in your life right now—every blessing, every responsibility, every opportunity. Write them down. See what's in your hands.

Third, What You've Received Isn't Yours, It's a Loan from God

One day you'll have to explain to God what you did with what you were given. In Jesus' story, after the master distributed the resources, he made it clear that he would eventually come back to see what they'd done with what belonged to him. They understood that the master would return and check on the status of his property. We need to grasp this also. Whatever resources, opportunities, and responsibilities you have came from God. One day, Jesus will return and you'll give an account of what you did with them.

Fourth, the Master Never Specifically Told the Servants What to Do with What They Had Been Given

Before the master departed, he didn't provide these servants with specific instructions. He didn't give them an investment seminar. The master didn't say, "Fellows, I want you to go and double my money!" He gave no instructions to them at all. Why not? Because it was a test. How do we know it was a test? Because he came back and graded them. Two of them received A+, and one of them failed. An important lesson in the story is that the master wanted to see what each of his servants would do with what they had been given, without any specific instructions provided.

These men had to decide for themselves how they would handle what was placed in their hands. They would determine what would happen with the gifts, opportunities, responsibilities, and resources provided. In other words, the owner wanted to see how much initiative, industriousness, and engagement they possessed, and how much effort they were willing to invest. He was testing their sense of responsibility, their understanding of stewardship, and their work ethic. But ultimately the master was testing the faithfulness of these men.

The same is true for you and me. God is watching what we do with what He's given to us. God doesn't do everything for us. He wants to see what *we'll* do—how much effort we'll bring to the table. While God is willing to work *for* us, He really wants to work w*ith* us and *through* us. The principle is clear: do what you can do, and God will do what only he can do. Become a partner with God. He wants to see how faithful you are. Do you just show up, or do you grow the thing assigned?

When the master in the story finally returned, it was accounting day. It's at this moment that we're able to see what the master really wanted from the three servants. When he called them together, it became clear that he was interested in how much progress they had made with the resources they had been given.

Of course, the two who multiplied what they had received were greatly commended. The one who maintained what he had received was condemned. The rebuke of the latter servant was not prompted by losing or decreasing what had been given him, it was prompted by the sad state of status quo—simply maintaining!

The lesson to us is obvious. God is looking for increase. Multiplication, growth, increase, productivity—all these things are part of what God expects from us as his servants. It's what marks us as faithful. It's what secures us commendations from God. It's what increases our spiritual joy.

Fifth, the Church Needs People Who Follow the Example of the Two Servants

The church desperately needs people in its workforce who understand the importance of *increasing*. People who are proactive, industrious, engaged, energetic, generous, and faith-filled in their Kingdom investments are incredible blessings.

People like this are always looking for ways to make their ministry teams better. They don't simply show up to do a job. They take ownership in the team. They look for ways to improve what they and their team members do. They look for new people to train and for new people to invite onto the team. They make their teams stronger and always leave them better. They don't have a negative, critical, grumbling, or griping spirit, but provide positive personal participation and contribution. They're disciplers, trainers, increasers, givers, helpers, fruit-bearers, and progress partners! They're up for any challenge and appreciative for any opportunity. They work together with God and others to accomplish the mission of building and growing his church.

As these qualities become more and more a part of you, you increasingly become a more productive part of the Kingdom team and a powerful, life-giving leader in the local church.

Multiplication Fact 4
The Apostle Paul Emphasized Multiplication

The fourth out of the five principles of multiplication is emphasized by the apostle Paul in one of his pastoral training manuals. In his second letter to Timothy, Paul gave him this advice: "You have heard me teach things that have been confirmed by many reliable witnesses. Now teach these truths to other trustworthy people who will be able to pass them on to others" (2 Timothy 2:2 NLT).

Paul told Timothy to take his responsibility as a multiplier seriously. He needed to increase the number of people doing the work of ministry in the local churches he oversaw. He was told to find people who understood the power and importance of multiplication so that the workload was distributed and the mission accomplishment was accelerated. Paul said, "Train people who will train people!"

Paul emphasized finding "trustworthy" or "faithful" people. What is faithfulness? Not simply showing up, but *multiplying*. Paul was saying, "Find the people who know how to multiply themselves. Find the people that have moved beyond doing to training. Find people who understand and value enlargement. Find faithful people who are willing and able to teach others."

In other words, Paul described the real work of leadership. Real leadership involves expansion. It involves more than just doing a ministry task. It includes influencing and training others to do the work of the ministry and to multiply themselves.

The church needs leaders—not just leaders that lead people, but leaders that inspire, build, and lead other leaders—leaders who multiply God's work in and through others. This kind of person realizes that what they have received from God should never *stop* with them, but should be expanded *through* them. This is a major part of what faithfulness is all about.

Multiplication Fact 5
The Impact of Multiplication Is Amazing

Multiplication is an amazing mathematical principle. It brings exponential increase. Here's a simple example of exponential power:

$2 \times 2 = 4$

$4 \times 4 = 16$

$16 \times 16 = 256$

$256 \times 256 = 65{,}536$

$65{,}536 \times 65{,}536 = 4.3$ million

In five steps, we go from four to 4,300,000. That's the principle of the exponential. That's why multiplication is so important. Its impact is astounding.

Think about the incredible possibilities of the advancement of God's Kingdom and his church if every believer, and certainly every servant of God in his church (and your church) were motivated to multiply. It's exhilarating to consider. All we have to do is *multiply.*

This is the vision God wants to put in your heart.

He wants you to be a fruitful believer, an increaser, a grower, a highly productive servant of God. He wants you to be motivated to multiply:

> If you have these qualities and they are increasing, it demonstrates that your knowledge about our Lord Jesus Christ is living and productive. (2 Peter 1:8 GW)

Power Points

- The value of growth is seen in God's very first commandment.
- Jesus taught multiplication.
- Multiplication is a measure of faithfulness.
- The apostle Paul emphasized multiplication.
- The impact of multiplication is amazing.

Power Prayer

Father, I thank you for this time together and for every person who has gone through this book.

I pray that the Holy Spirit will come upon each person and charge them up with vision to be encouragers and be increasers.

Put an excitement in their spirits, and a vision in their souls like they've never, ever had before. Let it search through their being.

Help them to make a difference wherever they are for the glory of God and the gospel of Jesus Christ,
in the name of Jesus, Amen.

ENDNOTES

1 "Attract." Merriam-Webster.com. Accessed August 15, 2016. http://www.merriam-webster.com/dictionary/attract.

2 "Assimilate." Merriam-Webster.com. Accessed August 15, 2016, http://www.merriam-webster.com/dictionary/assimilate.

3 "Alleviate." Merriam-Webster.com. AccessedAugust15,2016,http://www.merriam-webster.com/dictionary/alleviate.

4 Spiros Zodhiates, *Hebrew-Greek Key Study Bible.* (Chattanooga, Tenn.: AMG Publishers, 1984), 1683.

5 Sermon Index. "Proof (prove character, ordeal) (1382) docile." Accessed August 15, 2016. http://www.sermonindex.net/modules/articles/index.php?view=article&aid=34674].

6 Bible Hub. "1459.egkataleipó." Accessed August 15, 2016. http://biblehub.com/greek/1459.htm.

7 Albert Shaw, *Review of Reviews and World's Work, Volume 4* (Review of Reviews Corporation, 1892), 620, digitized April 9, 2010, accessed August 17, 2016; https://books.google.com/books?id=HLgrAQAAIAAJ&printsec=frontcover&source=gbs_ge_summary_r&cad=0#v=onepage&q&f=false.

8 Sloan Digital Sky Survey/SkyServer. "The Expanding Universe." Accessed July 30, 2016. http://skyserver.sdss.org/dr1/en/astro/universe/universe.asp.

Dale A. O'Shields

is the founding and senior pastor of Church of the Redeemer, a multi-cultural, multi-generational church with five campuses in the greater Washington, DC, area.

Pastor Dale is passionate about inspiring people to grow in Christ and impact their church and community. His practical teaching makes the Bible understandable and applicable in everyday life. His messages are broadcast widely and he has written several books and devotional resources. Pastor Dale invests in the next generation of church leaders through college-level classes and internship programs that prepare students for ministry through the local church.

In over thirty years of ministry, Pastor Dale has trained and equipped pastors, nationally and internationally, to plant and develop strong and thriving ministries. He founded the United Pastors Network to regularly invest in church leaders and teams.

Pastor Dale has been involved in pastoral ministry since 1978. He and his wife Terry have two married daughters and six grandchildren.

www.DaleOShields.com